Jennie Fowler Willing

Diamond Dust

Jennie Fowler Willing

Diamond Dust

ISBN/EAN: 9783743326835

Manufactured in Europe, USA, Canada, Australia, Japa

Cover: Foto ©ninafisch / pixelio.de

Manufactured and distributed by brebook publishing software (www.brebook.com)

Jennie Fowler Willing

Diamond Dust

Diamond Dust.

BY

MRS. JENNIE FOWLER WILLING,

AUTHOR OF "THROUGH THE DARK TO THE DAY," ETC.

CINCINNATI:
HITCHCOCK AND WALDEN.
NEW YORK: PHILLIPS & HUNT.
1880.

CONTENTS.

I.	Diamond Dust,	7
II.	Thinking,	37
III.	Married People,	77
IV.	Saving the Life,	109
V.	Courteousness,	135
VI.	My Neighbor,	157
VII.	How to get rid of "The Blues,"	178
VIII.	Getting Rich,	193
IX.	Giving by Rule,	207
X.	Growing Old,	222

Diamond Dust.

THERE are wonderful things to be seen in a watch factory; plucky little machines that bite off a steel bar with one snap of their jaws, discriminating little machines that handle screws one hundredth of an inch in length, exact little machines that measure the sixteenth of a hair's-breadth. But the one bit of mechanism that may most stir the thought is the tiny tin saw that cuts the jewels of the watch.

Yes, the delicate and difficult work of shaping the garnet and *aqua marina*, the ruby and sapphire, is done by a piece of *tin*—that soft, common metal. But notice! Its edge is charged with *diamond dust*.

Only the prince of gems can cut those precious stones. The diamond may not work alone. Its power must be made available through some cheaper agent to which it is joined. Probably the tin holds the diamond dust all the more tenaciously on account of its own weakness.

Why may not some noble, discouraged worker learn from the little tin saw how the jeweled pivots are cut, upon which turn the wheels of success in the world's conquest for God?

We are none of us content, unless we believe ourselves useful to others; and the broader our usefulness, the deeper and surer our peace. This principle sends delicate Christian women out of their snug homes, and sets them stumbling up into wretched attics, and down into dismal cellars. It sent scholarly Jesuits across the sea to freeze and starve among the North American Indians. Sometimes a rich, full life is poured out unstintedly in unselfish service, and with small result. The note of such a failure might almost send a throb of pain through an angel's song.

We all want to be useful. Children hear in a shell the moan of the sea. If we listen well, we can hear in the soul's confidences with itself a ceaseless moan for fellowship with God in his grand schemes of benevolence.

This universal bent indicates the divine intention. God uses human agents. He would use each of us to the limit of our powers, if we would meet the conditions of his inworking.

When we see those who are specially useful, we demand of ourselves to know why we are not doing more. Might not we accomplish something if only we could learn the secret of successful effort?

The earnest soul asks itself, "Have I found the line of life in which I can do most?" "Have I strength for any broader work than that which now occupies my time?"

It is plain that to work successfully we must find first, *what we can do best*, then satisfy ourselves that *our weakness is not a bar to success;* and learn, if we can, how the little tin saw we are set to manage can be *charged with the diamond dust of divine power.*

First, let us see *what God would have done.* We set our watches by the jeweler's chronometer because we want them right. It tells us where the sun is, and only the sun can give us standard time. If we would have right notions of God's work, the Sun of Divine Rightness must give us our standard. We must turn to the true Light that lighteth every man that cometh into the world.

We can be thoroughly useful only when we work the works of God. And what are they? To the Word and to the Testimony. From God's imperishable Record alone we may learn to what service we are to devote ourselves. Let us read carefully.

We find the stupendous miracle of creation

chronicled in a few lines, while chapter after chapter is given to warning, exhortation, and entreaty that wandering souls may be rescued from ultimate loss and death.

How simple is the story of the genesis of light, that wonderful effluence that makes possible all growth and beauty! How marvelous its movements! It puts its shoulder beneath all living things and lifts them toward the heavens in spite of the tremendous downward tug of gravitation. It brings note of suns so far away that a quarter of the life-time of the globe is needed to transmit the report. It pries into the minutest organism. It shows us the shuttles of life at work, weaving the living tissue; yet, marvelous as it is, the story of its birth is given us in a half-dozen words, though there is ample space to detail the penitence of a crucified thief, or the gratitude of a pardoned Magdalen.

We can be genuinely useful only when we work in line with the purpose of God. He renders the best service who does most to hasten the coming of the kingdom, be it by the conquest of an empire or the conversion of a child.

In seeking broad usefulness many blunder fatally. They mistake *éclat* for achievement, reputation for character, the huzzas of the crowd for the "Well done" of God. And they generally find what they seek. "Verily, verily, I say unto you, they have their reward." They climb up where the altitude is more lonely, the landscape more drear, and they become only a better mark for the peltings of the envious. They have a few years of pampered egotism and then an eternal stumbling upon the dark mountains of banishment from God.

Greatness usually comes to the door *a prince in disguise.* We keep the door closed and wait for the chariot and outriders that never come.

If we try to build for ourselves a pedestal that shall lift us into consequence, like children making cob palaces, our careless haste is constantly throwing down what we have set up; while, if we take some simple, humble work, and make of it all we possibly can, God working in us and with us, before we dream of such a thing it has grown to a height that lifts us into consideration.

In our personal salvation, we are forever stumbling over the simplicity of God's methods. We must have some marvelous revealment of the divine glory, some unbearable ecstasy, instead of the peace of Christ, the quiet faith-that believes his Word. Our diamond must blaze forth a Koh-i-noor, a mountain of light, and we push it aside with our foot, because it seems to our dull eyes only a common pebble. So our opportunity comes to us, not as a glorifying, but as a plain, unwelcome duty—a cross.

The line of life marked out for us by infinite wisdom is, of necessity, the very best possible.

Our weakness is not a bar to successful effort. The statement of the most logical and exact inspired writer is that God hath chosen the weak things of the world to confound the mighty. Not that he uses them when he can get no others, or when they are thrust in his way and he can not push them aside; but of all instruments, they are his choice; and the reason follows, "That no flesh may glory in his presence." He does not choose the weak because the strength of the strong is in his way, for the strongest are weak enough. These things are hid from the wise and prudent and revealed unto babes, because the wise and prudent will not take the attitude so natural and easy for the babes.

Tin is chosen instead of the richer metals to hold the diamond dust on account of its very poverty.

God always uses means utterly inadequate to the result to be produced, that it may be thoroughly understood that the excellency of the power is not of men, but of himself. Then needy souls will know that to him alone they must look as the source of help and strength. and not to the servants that do his bidding.

God's use of inadequate means may be seen in the material world.

When he makes an oak, he does not speak it into being by a word of power; he wraps the embryo in an insignificant nut, and drops it upon the ground. A foot presses it into the soil. The frost gnaws at its shell. Life touches the germ and sets the "bioplasts" at work. They begin to weave an oak, and presently its tiny leaflets push their way through the ground, and up toward the light. The nip of a lambkin might destroy the little vegetable, but, guarded by the law of the survival of the fittest, it climbs away upward till its forehead is among the clouds. That immense, upright column of wood is all from the tiny embryo.

When God would send a river forth on its mission of power and use and beauty, he does not open one of the earth's great arteries, and pour a mighty flood down the mountain side. A few drops trickle from beneath a stone. A baby's touch might turn the runlet this way or that. It slips away through grass and mosses till it catches a song in its heart, and dances over a pebbly bed, a thing of beauty and of gladness.

Joining hands with kindred rills, it grows in power, gathering in its arms other streams, till at last it rolls in might toward the ocean, bearing on its bosom the inland commerce of a people.

When a continent is to be made, the Great Architect does not set the Titans hammering the mountains about under the sea, that he may lay its base-stones. He gives the order to a tiny polyp that lives but a day; and presently the coral reef is thrown across the path of navigation. Then the island lifts its head above the wave, and soon the continent becomes the home of races of living beings.

The ocean lies still and quiet in its rocky bed, its deep heart unmoved by the tornadoes that thunder across its surface, tossing great navies hither and thither like handfuls of feathers. Yet, under the moonbeam's kiss, it lifts tons and tons of its waters from their place and throws them for leagues along the shore.

Gravitation is a law so delicate that philosophers fumbled around it for centuries without being able to find it; yet it is so mighty that, by it the Creator holds the universe in balance.

The Master seems to have wrought by this rule of the use of inadequate means in his redemptive and reformatory work. In his miracles he used means looking toward the end desired, yet always unequal to the result. His mightiest marvels were wrought by a word or a touch. When the multitude followed him out of their homes, so eager to hear the Word that they lost sight of their physical needs, he told his disciples to give them food. He could have spoken into being a Himalaya of bread; but then the great lesson of the miracle would have been lost. He took the five loaves and the two small fishes, and blessed, and brake, and set the doubters catering for the great rows of hungry people. Each took his pitiful bit of bread, and stumbled toward those whom he was to serve with a thousand keen eyes watching his movements. He broke off each piece in faith, and there was no lessening of the supply, for the creative power of him who issued the command was brought into requisition by obedient trust.

In the work of grace, the Lord Jesus Christ always wrought by the same rule. He committed the tremendous work of the world's conquest to a little company of Galilean peasants, though he might have chosen Judean rabbis, Athenian philosophers, or Roman poets and statesmen, or he might have called to his aid legions of angels. He left his work in the hands of a few fisher people, uncouth in manners, burry in speech, untrained in thought, with little to commend them to confidence, except their sterling sense and their faith in his power.

Indeed, the entire scheme of salvation is based upon a contradiction of common opinions, diametrically opposed to all that the world believes requisite to success. Its vital point is trust in the crucified Nazarene. No wonder that it should be foolishness to the philosophic Greeks and a stumbling-block to the aristocratic, hierarchal Jews.

In all time the great advance movements of reform have been by the use of means that had, of necessity, to be supplemented by divine power.

During the dark ages, when a woman was a being to be treated with silly adulation or contempt, a plaything or a drudge, altogether unfit to be trusted with a knowledge of books or of affairs, even in those murky days, a woman was used for the evangelization of nearly every country in Europe.

Helena, the mother of Constantine the Great, made Christianity the religion of the Roman Empire, and so of the civilized world.

The Empress Olga brought Christianity into Russia; and her grandson, Vladimir the Great, who established it as the religion of the empire, was converted through the agency of his wife, Anna of Constantinople.

Hungary was brought to Christ through the efforts of Sarolta, a Christian princess, wife of King Geysa, and mother of St. Stephen.

The Poles were converted under the reign of Micislas I, through the influence of his Christian wife, Dambrouska. Olaf the Good, who became the apostle of Scandinavia, carrying the leaven of evangelism even to Iceland and Greenland, was the convert of his wife, Gyda. Our own British ancestors were indebted for the permanent establishment of Christianity among them to the efforts of good Queen Bertha.

In the sixteenth century, a few earnest Germans were praying that the emperor might be aroused to stand for the old spirituality that had been so nearly trampled out by papal aggression, and the answer came in the conversion of a miner's scape-grace son.

While in the depths of despair the mighty doctrine of justification by faith dawned upon Luther's dark soul; and that belief of an obscure monk was God's engine for laying as level as the walls of Jericho the old bastions of papal power in Germany.

Poor, alone, persecuted, he stood before the potentates of the empire at Worms with the simple, sturdy answer to the command to recant: "*Hier stehe Ich, Ich kann nicht anders. So hilf mir Gott. Amen."* When he was buried in the Wartburg out of the reach of friend and foe, he wrought the great work of the Reformation, the translation of the Bible into the speech of the people. In that work he gave Germany her language. Lifting a dialect into a speech by translating into it the Scriptures, he made a vehicle of thought that rendered possible the marvelous German literature that has followed. Greater still, he made permanent the Reformation. Always and ever the greatest is evolved from the least.

The Anglican revival of the eighteenth century was born in an obscure rectory, where a woman was holding her nineteen children to a regimen as rigorous as that of West Point, and yet so gentle and tender, Dr. Clarke says, they had the reputation of being the most loving family in the county of Lincoln.

With a verse-making, wool-gathering husband who had not practical sense enough to keep out of jail for debt, she not only looked well to the ways of her household, but she helped her boys with their classics, and through the intricacies of their religious experience. Little thought she as the days went on, crowded to the last second with infinitesimal cares, that she was laying the foundation of the greatest revival of spiritual godliness that these later centuries have witnessed. Little did even the wisest imagine that in that obscure rectory a moral renovation was being planned that was to change the life of millions—possibly even the polity of all civilized nations—piercing with its darts of light the gloom above all races the wide world over. Lay preaching has been the driving-wheel of the Wesleyan machinery. When God set it spinning, John Wesley's high-church prejudices made him unequal to the test. He came home from one of his itinerant tours, and, finding out what had been set on foot in his absence, he said to his mother, with unusual asperity, "So, Thomas Maxfield has turned preacher!" "Yes, and do you be careful how you lay your hand on that young man. He is just as certainly called of God to preach as you are." She kept him from throwing the band off the driving-wheel.

When God thrust Wesley out to preach upon the moors and commons to the masses that could not be gathered into the churches to hear the Word, a storm of persecution arose and church doors were slammed in his face. His mother steadied his courage, "Never mind, my son, the work is of God. Go on, and leave results with him." She stood by his side, that gray-haired old mother, when he spoke upon

Kennington Common to twenty thousand people. But for that small and often overlooked factor, the mother's faith, where would have been the great scheme of evangelism?

The Sabbath-school is unequaled in its power for the spread of the Gospel among the masses. Its beginning was humble enough. In 1769 Hannah Ball established a Sunday-school in Wycombe, England. Twelve years later another young woman, who afterwards became the wife of Samuel Bradburn, a celebrated lay preacher, suggested to Robert Raikes the idea of teaching the children the Word of God, and she walked with him through the streets of Gloucester when he went to the church with his little, ragged company to try the first experiment. The people hooted at the woman's whim, but "the handful of corn upon the top of the mountains, the fruit thereof shakes like Lebanon."

At the beginning of this century the Chinese Empire was closed against Christian truth. Its language, the speech of nearly half the people of the world, was without even a touch of Christian literature. A Sunday-school teacher induced a street boy to come into her class. She gave him suitable clothing and he came one Sunday. The next he was missing. She hunted him up, clothed him again, and brought him again to the school. He came only one Sabbath and disappeared again. She persevered and the third time she succeeded in holding him in her class. A trifling matter, to be sure, but that boy was Robert Morrison, who became the apostle to China, opening that vast empire to the Gospel of Christ.

The American Board of Commissioners of Foreign Missions, belting the world with its successful work, grew out of the talk of some college boys sitting beside a hay-stack one Saturday afternoon, where they had taken refuge from a shower. They talked of the heathen and of the possibility of their conversion, and agreed to meet regularly to pray for the salvation of the pagan world, and out of that prayer-meeting grew the American Board.

The Methodist Missionary Society, with its broad fields and noble workers, grew out of the effort of a little company of women who banded together and began work by sending a negro to teach the Indians upon the Western Reserve.

But time would fail to speak of all the great schemes that God has inaugurated through the smallest agencies. Indeed, such a catalogue would cover the greater part of the divine work in the world, as this method is the rule instead of the exception.

The Jews stumbled to their utter ruin over

the simple, unpretentious coming of their Prince Messiah, the Desire of Nations. The reputed son of a carpenter, unheralded, except by the signs that accompanied his birth, why should they acknowledge his claim? During his thirty years of waiting he moved about among them simply a thoughtful, young man, with sad, patient eyes, differing from others only in probity, which was any thing but a passport to distinction, saying strange, wise things, but never bringing to pass any thing remarkable.

He waited in insignificance and obscurity while the great world—His world—known to him in its ultimate atoms, turned silently on its axis, kissed by his sunbeams, touched by his frosts, enriched by the rains that he sent upon the evil and the good, its people filling their cup of condemnation.

At last His hour struck, and he stepped to the front, putting his shoulder to the mighty work of redemption. But even then he was unknown to Greek scholarship, unheard of in that magnificent city of the Cæsars. Probably not a thinker in those superb old Indian and Chinese empires pronounced his name. He lived in a remote Roman province, hated and persecuted, and he died at last a felon's death. But Richter says of him, "He who was the holiest among the mighty, and the mightiest among the holy has, with his pierced hand, lifted heathenism off its hinges, and turned the dolorous and accursed centuries into new channels, and now governs the ages."

Since it appears plainly that our weakness is no bar to successful work for God, how shall we get about it to have our weak human nature charged with the diamond dust of divine power?

1. We must understand *our own weakness*. This is the Sebastopol of the campaign, the key to the position.

The Master said, "Without me ye can do nothing." He understood our puerile attempts at bolstering our own dignity. He knew how hard we would try to make ourselves and others believe that we were equal to the work in hand. He meant we should begin with a sense of utter inefficiency. Frederic the Great, with a little of the insight of genius, said that the three hardest words to pronounce are, "I was mistaken."

We may be too polite to trumpet our own doings. We may have more sense than Longfellow's Iago.

> "Very boastful was Iago.
> Never heard he an adventure,
> But himself had met a greater;
> Never any deed of daring,
> But himself had done a bolder;

Never any marvelous story,
But himself could tell a stranger."

Yet if we watch ourselves we will find that always, if we can, we turn the conversation away from those topics upon which we appear to disadvantage, and toward those that show off our achievements. It comes so easy to say, "When I was in the university," or, "When we were abroad," or, "When their High Mightinesses, So and So, were at our house."

While we are filled with a sense of our own importance, we can not be partakers of the divine nature so as to be full of power by the Spirit of the Lord.

We must not only be converted, we must become as little children.

There is an inborn spirit of independence that must be gotten rid of as soon as possible.

When Thales was asked what is the most difficult thing in the universe, he replied, "To know thyself." So tricky are we, we hide our real motives even from our closest self-scrutiny. We practice hypocrisy upon ourselves even when we are airing our sincerity and ingenuousness.

We intone our confession of unworthiness with proper inflections and cadences. We are poor, miserable sinners, but not unfrequently our drawl of humility covers self-assertion as a wet cloth covers a dead man's face, making it all the more ghastly to them who have eyes.

If somebody agrees with us in our declarations of incompetency, we catch ourselves suddenly straightening our vertebral column, and asserting stiffly that we are probably quite as wise and good as the majority of our neighbors. Much of the discipline of life is meant to make us see this defect of character.

How plainly we see the independence of the little fellow toddling off on his two uncertain feet. If he can push open the gate he starts out wildly toward any point of the compass in the big outside world, and how resolutely he resists with kicks and screams every attempt to force him back within safe and proper limits.

If a mother leaves her little girl in charge of the house she is sure to find that the child forgot to feed the chickens and keep the pigs out of the garden, in her disastrous attempts to show that she can make pies and clean house all by herself.

Older people dislike to be told to do what they think they understand as well as any body.

"You had better take your shawl, Mary; it will be cool coming home."

"No, mother, I sha'n't need it."

When we were upon the sidewalk, the young

lady, who was more thoughtful in her introspection than most people, asked this question, "Why do you suppose I told mother I did n't need my shawl, when I meant to take it all the time, and should have done so if she had n't spoken about it—just as though I did n't know enough to take care of my health?"

You are in a street-car that gets into some sort of trouble. "Do n't be frightened," says a superior individual with that soothing cadence that is specially provoking. "Just sit still, there's no danger." You are on your feet in a moment. You are no baby. You probably know as well as he how to behave, danger or no danger.

This personal *hauteur* is probably a remnant of the original human kingliness. But whatever it is, it is sadly in the way of good work, for before honor is humility.

Before we can be properly equipped for the divine service, we must know thoroughly that we are utterly helpless for good, except as God becomes the strength of our strengthlessness.

Only God has power to help souls to a better life. He is jealous for the divine prerogative, not for his own sake, but for ours.

A jeweler will not let his little boy tamper with a watch, no matter how dear the child may be to his heart. Not because he is afraid that his son may become a rival in business, but because he is afraid the little fellow will ruin the watch, if allowed to get at its wheels and ratchets.

We know so little of the human spirit we can never be sure of saying or doing the right thing for its helping, except as our Father holds our hand, and speaks through our lips.

There is an aloneness of grandeur about this awful human soul. It may be trampled in mire like a lost diamond; it may be built into coarse, common wall like the broken, scattered Greek marbles, but an archangel would stand back abashed from the audacity of laying unbidden so much as the weight of a finger upon the delicate, immense mechanism.

Shall we be so foolhardy as to attempt any reformatory work, except simply and only as instruments in the divine hand?

When we get out of the swaddling bands of our selfhood, we are brought face to face with the ultimate facts of being, and character, and destiny, the dignity of the soul and its final future, and we become indifferent to our own apparent success or failure, so that the work in which we are permitted a part moves forward.

2. We must have a sense of *God's adequacy to the work in hand.*

> "For right is right, since God is God,
> And right the day must win.
> To doubt would be disloyalty,
> To falter would be sin."

In the Sacred Record we find that those who asked and received great things of God usually prefaced their prayer with a statement of the divine greatness. That, as I understand it, was not that they might propitiate the Deity by an ascription of praise, for the best human attempts to tell him who and what he is must be to his ear mere limping, childish chirping. They said these things that their own minds might be saturated with the thought of his power, and the ease with which he could deliver them from troubles that seemed so great.

Thus, when Hezekiah was in mortal terror before the coming of Sennacherib's host, he prayed before the Lord, and said: "O Lord of hosts, God of Israel, which dwellest between the cherubim, thou art the God, even thou alone, of all the kingdoms of the earth. Thou hast made heaven and earth."

After the ascension of the Lord, when the little company of disciples found themselves precipitated by their faith into a most unequal contest with the authorities, they cried to God for help. With the fires of martyrdom beginning to scorch their faces, they felt intensely the need of a strong refuge; so they began their prayer by saying: "Lord, thou art God, which hast made heaven and earth and the sea and all that in them is," and immediately their faith touched the Divine Hand in the darkness, and the place where they were was shaken by his presence.

3. We must commit ourselves to the *Divine guidance.*

There is such a tangle of paths before us, only one of which can be right, we are often bewildered to know what course to take. No human plummet can sound the abyss of difficulty. No human strength can bridge the chasm.

Like Solomon, when he stood in the presence of the tremendous responsibilities of life, we say: "I am a little child, I know not how to go out or to come in." Our Heavenly Father sees the end from the beginning, and we have his promise, "In all thy ways acknowledge him, and he shall direct thy paths." He will lead us, probably not to that that will bring money or luxury, *éclat* or self-indulgence. If those accidents of life are in the way of a broad usefulness, we renounce them all, and he will save us from their allurements.

John Wesley, the retiring, poetic, studious Oxonian, was led away from the quiet, scholarly life he would have chosen, to one packed with public cares and burdens and self-denials. For twenty long years he endured that miserable thorn in the flesh, a jealous, unprincipled wife. For half a century his Church bore down upon him with her broadsides of persecution, his brethren in holy orders usually leading the attack. When his followers had become so numerous that he had to be treated with a little leniency, he was afraid something had gone wrong with him, because he missed the mobs.

The Apostle Paul was also of that fine, gentle, scholastic cast of mind that shuns notoriety and enjoys so intensely cloistered leisure with books. He was led of God in journeyings often, in perils of waters, in perils of robbers, in perils by his own countrymen, in perils by the heathen, in perils in the city, in perils in the wilderness, in perils in the sea, in perils among false brethren, in weariness and painfulness, in watchings often, and, at last, he went to his throne from beneath the headsman's sword.

The Lord Christ was a man of sorrows and acquainted with grief. He did not of himself choose the suffering, for he cried out during that supreme hour of anguish in Gethsemane, "If it be possible, let this cup pass from me; nevertheless, not my will but thine be done."

We can not pierce the awful mystery of that redemptive agony. He staggered through its surges of anguish, grappling with and mastering the powers of evil. He was heard in that he feared, and his dying cry, "It is finished," was a victor's shout. The cross was his throne of triumph and it is our symbol of victory.

We must drop into the little niche in the divine plan for which we were designed. We can work to advantage only when we move in harmony with the Unerring Will.

4. We must have *faith for results*.

God means at the earliest possible hour to set this wrong old world right. If we are in his hand, under his control, there is no possible chance for us to fail.

> "Ill with his blessing is most good,
> And unblest good is ill;
> And all is right that seems most wrong,
> If it is his dear will."

They of whom the world was not worthy, who subdued kingdoms, wrought righteousness, obtained promises, stopped the mouths of lions, quenched the violence of fire, escaped the edge of the sword, out of weakness were made strong, waxed valiant in fight, and turned to flight the armies of the aliens, wrought all their marvels by faith. But how can we attain "like precious faith?"

The Savior asked, "How can ye believe which receive honor one of another, and seek not the honor that cometh from God only."

One of the first conditions upon which we may hope for the enlarged faith that is so important a factor in successful work for God is the renunciation of our desire for the approbation of others. That, however, is but one point of the complete self-surrender that is necessary. There must be a choice of the will of God in all things for all time. This must be as complete as we know how to make. Every suggestion of possible service or suffering must be met with, "Yes, if it be his will, I will do it. I can trust him to keep me out of fanaticism and unnecessary self-mortification. I simply put the conduct of my life into his hands."

We must understand that the immanent God has a will in every item of our life, and the only safe and wise thing is for us to choose that will, no matter how our inclination may writhe and struggle and cry out in pain.

Once when Marshal Ney was going into battle he noticed that his knees were smiting together from fear. Looking down at them, he said: "You may well shake. You'd shake worse yet if you knew where I am going to take you!" That was Ney holding Ney in the line of duty, in spite of terror that curdled the blood, and it was by that resolute choice of right action that he earned the title of the "bravest of the brave."

But how may we know that we are not cheating ourselves, that we do in all things choose the will of God, that our surrender to him is complete?

We know whether or not we are honest in our purpose to do this; and when we are reminded of the depth and deceitfulness of the human heart, we may reply, "I know that the Holy Spirit, to whom I am indebted even for my desire to be wholly under his control, and who knows my motives to their last shade of meaning,—is able, and cares to show me, if I fail of a complete surrender. I am so sure of this, I venture to say to my friends, to every body, if need be, I know through my confidence in his helping power that I am wholly given to God."

After that it is easy to believe that he has you in his hand, and he works in you to will and to do of his good pleasure the condition necessarily antecedent to your greatest usefulness.

You may assert by faith in the blood of the everlasting covenant that he saves from the old egotism and fits the soul for the best work for himself.

The soul "enters into rest," profound, sweet, holy. There is no further care about the choice of work. God, to whom the life is committed, will lead by his spirit so that all things shall work together for good. The responsibility of result is all with God. There is nothing to do but to go on gladly, trustfully, doing to the best of the ability what he would have done, leaving the outcome with him.

The suffrage of the world and the "Well done" of God are given finally to those who work by this rule of submission and trust.

"Count me o'er earth's chosen heroes; they were souls that stood alone,
While the men they agonized for hurled the contumelious stone,
Stood serene, and down the future saw the golden beam incline
To the side of perfect justice mastered by their faith divine,
By one man's plain truth to manhood and to God's supreme design.

By the light of burning heretics Christ's bleeding feet I track,
Toiling up new Calvaries ever with the cross that turns not back.
And these mounts of anguish number how each generation learned
One new word of that grand *credo* which in prophet-hearts hath burned,
Since the first man stood God-conquered with his face to heaven upturned.

For humanity sweeps onward: where to-day the martyr stands,
On the morrow crouches Judas, with the silver in his hands,
Far in front the cross stands ready and the crackling fagots burn,
While the hooting mob of yesterday in silent awe return
To glean up the scattered ashes for history's golden urn."

A picture of Florence Nightingale represents her by the bedside of a dying soldier in a Crimean hospital. In the background a poor, homesick fellow has raised himself in his cot and is passing his hand caressingly, reverently over her shadow on the opposite wall—rendering unconscious homage to her boundless self-giving.

A friend wrote her once, asking for some facts of her life for publication. Her reply was about this: "There is nothing worth writing about me. I have done nothing, God has done all. He has been pleased to take a very plain, ordinary woman and use her in his service. I have worked hard, very hard, and I have never denied God any thing."

Of another of the mighty ones whose weak life was so charged with the diamond dust of divine power that it cut through adamantine mountains of difficulty, the record is, "Abraham believed God, and he counted it to him for righteousness." Stanley says: "Powerful as is the effect of these words when we read them in their first untarnished freshness, they gain immensely in their original language, to which neither Greek nor German, much less Latin or English, can furnish any full equivalent. 'He was supported, he was built up, he reposed as a child in its mother's arms' [such seems the force of the Hebrew word] in the strength of God."

And this is the privilege of every believer in the Lord Jesus Christ. That the weapons of our warfare may be so edged and driven by divine power as to be mighty through God to the pulling down of strongholds, we must have the sense of utter personal weakness, and of omnipotent help that comes only from complete obedience and restful trust.

THINKING.

THE demand of the time is for trained thinking. The great need of God's work is consecrated thought.

We desire to be broadly useful. We attempt many things in which we fail. Our failures throw us into the deepest humiliation and despondency. We have seasons of resolving to be intensely vigilant and active, followed by corresponding lapses into unprofitableness. We never are, but always are to be, of some use in the world. Unless something changes the current and character of our effort, the chances are that old age or death will find us like some convocations of well meaning people, resolving and resolving, "only that and nothing more."

Perhaps the clew that will lead us out of this labyrinth of failures may be found to be a habit of direct, sure thought under God's guidance.

An item of advice given by the London admiralty to its seamen in regard to the management of a ship in a hurricane begins with this sentence; "Stand erect and look in the wind's eye." It may be well for us to stand erect and look in the eye the difficulties that hold us from our best possible achievement. If we find the trouble to lie in our slipshod, zigzag methods of thought, let us do our best to amend.

An earnest glance at the world's affairs will convince us that thinking pays. It increases the mental volume. The more we do in any line, the more we can do. It is the arm that works that has muscle and vigor. It is the brain that thinks that has power to think to good purpose.

Thinking has a *market value*. Deft fingers are worth far more in a business than clumsy ones are; and even in what seems simply to depend on physical skill, success hinges upon the quickness and sureness of the thought. There is no appreciable difference in the quality of the muscle, or blood, or nerve in the cunning or the awkward hand. The difference is in the mind that directs the movements of each. Success in any avocation is not usually a matter of special endowment, but of disciplined thought.

What makes the difference in the wages of those who go out to service? You have a servant whom you have to tell but once how you want a thing done. She understands and remembers. Her work is worth a dollar a week more than that of another who brings to you as pleasant ways, larger experience, and more muscle, but who is forever forgetting or neglecting some important item of home comfort. You can well afford to pay the thoughtful housekeeper all she chooses to ask for her services. Her planning, "executive force," as we sometimes call it, adds at least one-half to her availability. Her thoughtfulness is of no small value to you, if it leaves you free to use your thought upon other and possibly more important matters, though it is not easy to believe that any business can be more important than that the home be kept as it ought to be. Many a failure is due to the ill-temper and the nervous unhingement caused by a smoky breakfast-room, burnt steak, or cold cakes.

In mechanical operations the question of financial success hinges upon the formula, the more thought, the better pay. If one thinks nimbly and strongly enough to keep the muscles of two others at work, he becomes three men. If a hundred, he multiplies his producing force a hundred times; and in just so far as he can think out the work of others better than they can do it for themselves, he is entitled to profit on their work. That is the way in which honest men get rich. If one can plan so that the strength of another is worth as much again as it would be without his thought, he is entitled to a share of the extra gains. That is fair. The thought field is open to all. If one wants the better paying position, let him learn also to think rapidly and reliably.

It is hard work to learn thinking, but it renders the best returns to all classes of workers, from the bootblack trying to establish his respectability by presenting a clean face in the Mission school, up to Bismarck and Disraeli playing their cosmopolitan game, with kings and emperors for chessmen.

Great achievements are not accidental. They are the result of tireless thought.

It was not the genius of a demi-god that so nearly laid Europe at the feet of the great Napoleon. It was the ceaseless energy of a herculean thinker. While other men slept, he would sit by the hour bending over his maps, and planning his campaigns. With colored pins he represented the forces in the contest. The green pins were Russians, the blue pins Prussians, the red pins the British, and the white pins his own soldiers. If the allied armies were to move upon a certain point, he would bring up his men by forced marches to its relief. If they crossed the river here, he would fall back so and so. Thus through the livelong night in that great, tough brain, armies were marching and counter-marching, and those plans were wrought out that astonished the world with the brilliancy of their success.

It holds true of every enterprise, whether it be for Satan, or self, or God; its success, other things being equal, depends upon the amount of clear, definite, *continuous thought* that is given to its planning and execution. If one would work well, he must learn to think well.

Few people study their mental movements carefully enough to understand their lack of ability for sustained thought.

One may test himself by watching his attempts at listening to a lecture. He seats himself with a determination to give his very best attention to the subject in hand. After two or three minutes some word of the speaker reminds him of a teacher of his, and in a twinkling he is in the old New England school-house, with the boys buzzing and shuffling and playing sly tricks. John Smith used to sit by him. Poor John! He was killed in that Ashtabula disaster. What a terble thing that was, to be sure. He would have been in it if he hadn't lain over in Rochester. That trip to San Francisco was lucky all the way through. What a set those Chinese are that he saw there. How queer it would seem to be in China where all the people look like those odd specimens. He is called home from the Celestial Empire, not by the subject under discussion, but by a bustling step at his side—Doctor Dosem! Wonder if he is as busy as he tries to make out! He has lost a good slice of the lecture by coming so late. The lecture! Shades of the Greeks! If that lecturer has not reached his thirdly, and not a word of secondly has caught the erratic attention of this average listener!

Let him test himself in another way. Let him resolve to think steadily for ten minutes upon any given subject, whether it be the care of his health, the salvation of his soul, or any other vital matter. He will find his thought wandering like the eyes of a fool to the ends of the earth. If so much as a fly buzzes near, it will snap the gossamer thread of his thought and set it flying a thousand leagues from the subject in hand.

How can we *learn to think* continuously and rapidly? How can this rickety, lumbering, unreliable thinking-machine be put in such repair that it can be depended upon to do a given amount of work in a given time, and not waste nine-tenths of its force in dawdling?

We learn thinking by thinking. Practice makes perfect. A little girl can not learn to make the thread go directly through the eye of her needle till she has thrust it this side and that at least a thousand times. She can not learn to take up the proper amount of cloth at each stitch, and set each stitch beside the one nearest to which it belongs, till she has pricked her finger to roughness in false passes.

A boy does not learn skating from lectures on that pastime, but by buckling on the skates and testing his ability to retain the perpendicular. He learns to let the center of gravity fall within the base from the penalty attending an infraction of that law, in the way of an emphatic bump on the ice now and then.

We send our boys and girls to school, and they are crowded through declensions and paradigms day after day, not that by and by they are to earn a livelihood by repeating those intricate and bewildering linguistic differences, but they will need in any business the steady, straight thinking that can be developed only by these and similar exercises.

When they venture out upon the glare ice of their lyceum argumentations and other wit contests, we clap hands and cry, "Bravo!" We know that they are learning the use of their metaphysical skates as certainly while their feet are gyrating through the air, and they are measuring their length in an intellectual tumble, as when they astonish lookers-on with wonderful evolutions in the mental rink.

How can we train ourselves to *direct thinking?* Shall we choose a subject and sit down with a determination to lash ourselves over a given line for a given time, till we learn to go through the exercise properly? By no means. Our minds would resent such treatment and play us any number of shabby tricks, rather than submit to the arbitrary discipline. They would be as intractable as little girls whom antiquated maidens oblige to sew seams of infinite length and tediousness by flourishing homilies over their heads, instead of beguiling the tiresome monotony by some pretty story or sentiment. We would rebel so resolutely against the exercise that a nervous fever or something worse would be the result.

There must be something about which we think while we are learning to think that seems, for the time at least, to be worth the effort. There needs to be usually the social element enabling us to compare our work and progress with that of others, and receive stimulus from emulation and appreciation. Few are earnest and patient enough to work their way alone through the memorizing of the terminology of a science or language. It can be done, however, and it must be held as a *dernier ressort* in case one is deprived of the helps of teachers and class drill that are found in college study.

If one is young enough the best thing is to take a *collegiate course.* Poverty is no excuse in this land where colleges are so numerous and democratic. If we set out upon a course of mental drill we will find it takes all the energy of the faculty with their "honors" and "standing" and every motive they can bring to bear upon us to keep us at work. So lawless are we by nature, it will seem the supreme happiness to escape from the grinding machinery and turn Modoc or Arab or any body who does not have to study. The more our school work annoys us, the more certainly do we need it, and the more resolutely must we determine to drive or wheedle or coax ourselves through its drudgery.

But suppose we are too old or too heavy-laden to go to school? What then? Let us set before us the example of the learned blacksmith and others who have done wonders in this line, even while earning their living at hard labor. Let us remember that all things are possible,

"Heart within and God o'erhead."

Let us mark out *an easy line of study* that we can hold evenly, and then let us not turn aside for any thing.

I knew a woman who had the care of her house, doing all its work without help, and aiding her husband in his ministerial duties as far as she could, yet she managed to acquire the equivalent of a college course, and much besides. She swept her house to the rhythm of Tennyson and Longfellow. She bent over her ironing-board with a German grammar open beside her work, and repeated, *Ich bin, du bist, er ist,* while she smoothed the sheets and pillow-cases. She crowded her house care into the closest possible compass—without robbing the home of its comfort—that she might get time to study. That of itself was an excellent exercise. Along at first she gave only fifteen minutes a day to the language or science she was busy upon; but she kept a close account with herself, and if, by any chance, she lost the fifteen minutes, she made up the time as soon as the company was gone or the obstacle removed. By thus obliging herself to perform a given amount of work each day she was preparing herself for heavier duties in the future; and by saving the fragments of time she was acquiring the means for the better discipline and enrichment of her mind.

In learning to think, *What shall we study?* We may answer in general terms, Just what we do not want to study. Each line of mental exercise is meant to develop the powers in a certain direction. If a given line is easy and agreeable, it is quite certain that one has already the development that would be the result of that discipline. For instance, *linguistic drill* gives quickness, nimbleness of thought. If one translates readily from one language into another, he is obliged to spring from one to the other with the utmost rapidity. You are talking to a German. You think "house," but, before you can recall its German equivalent, the French *"maison"* that you learned in your childhood thrusts itself forward impertinently and almost drops from your tongue tip. You dart back and rummage a drawer full of Greek and Latin odds and ends. Something suggests the kinship between the English and German, and, the ear getting a chance to give a hint, you bring out the word you are looking for—*"haus."* That portion of duration called time has been gliding along all this while, and, as in a beginner's practice upon the piano, there are such long pauses between the objective points, your speaking is any thing but concise and correct.

When the student of music learns to think rapidly enough to get his perception of the note in the printed lesson telegraphed to his hand, bringing his finger down upon the right key, with no appreciable loss of time or style, we vote him accomplished. So when one is able to change the thought that comes to him in his vernacular into another language without waiting to hunt up the word he needs to use, we know that his mind acts readily, his thought is nimble. If one is specially fond of the study of languages, so that all that work is easy for him, he has already what he would acquire from such drill.

As nimbleness is not usually compatible with strength and steadiness, one who can translate readily may decide that his mind needs a discipline that will give it the ability for sustained effort. That discipline is usually found in *mathematical study.*

Not that there is any thing in mental contact with numbers that specially stimulates or strengthens the mind, but success in mathematical work depends largely upon continuous attention. In general study you can continue the mechanical effort while your mind is prancing about leagues away from the subject in hand. It is difficult to detect its erratic movements; but in mathematical study, when one is trying to solve a difficult problem, if he looks aside from the mark for even thirty seconds, the chances are he will have to go back and go over all the ground again to find the clew he has dropped. He is like one drawing up a bucket of water with a rope hand over hand. If he lets the rope go for half a minute, the bucket will fall and all his labor be wasted.

Study, like that of mathematics, that enables one to know whether or not he is holding his attention steadily upon the matter before him, is the best exercise to give a habit of going straight through the mental work in hand. Lord Bacon says: "There is no stand or impediment in the wit but may be wrought out by fit studies. If a man's wit be wandering let him study mathematics; for in demonstrations, if his wit be called away never so little, he must begin again; so every defect of mind may have a special receipt."

In the ordinary avocations of life we have little use for any mathematical knowledge beyond the simple rules of arithmetic, yet we need in every thing the habit of thinking steadily and continuously.

For instance, one is buying a home. He is making up his mind upon the merits of a certain piece of property. He must consider the economy of the purchase, his ability to meet the payments, the health of the place, its neighborhood, schools, society, growth, and a dozen other items that are vital to the plan.

Other things being equal, the man or woman who can go straight through the details of a business transaction, as he would have to do through a difficult mathematical problem to find its solution, is the one who can manage his affairs with skill and success. The one who lacks this ability to think abstractly and consecutively will get his attention caught on some pleasant feature of the bargain, and will lose sight of a disadvantage that the one with whom he is dealing may spare no pains to hide.

In buying even a piece of furniture a woman goes through the same mental processes that are necessary to the solution of a difficult problem in calculus. The main difference is, if she loses her way in the problem she knows it at once, and goes back to find the path again, but in the business of settling the domestic and social details of her home she may lose her way in the reasoning and fail of the right conclusions, and not know it until her affairs are in a hopeless tangle, and an interest of priceless worth has made shipwreck. A slight error in nautical calculation sent the *Atlantic* upon the rocks with its hundreds of human lives. Many a well-freighted home craft has gone down in a sullen sea, because the one at the helm failed to think steadily and surely through the problem of its management.

In a saloon fray in the cañons of Colorado, the vital question, which of the ruffians shall go out upon his feet and which shall be carried out upon a shutter, depends upon the quickness with which the muscle of the trigger finger obeys the will. We may be sure the men who live that desperate life keep themselves well up in pistol practice. We come to places where every thing depends upon our thought going as swift and sure as a minie-ball through the problem of destiny. There is no time for practice, no room for bungling. In an instant the chance has flashed by—the doom is sealed.

The young man who clung to a capsized skiff, while the waves of Lake Michigan tossed him hither and thither the livelong night, found that his life depended upon the reserve power of his muscle, his ability to hold on amid the beating of the surges where others would have let go and sunk in death.

That friend of mine who held her nerves quiet while she cowed a fierce dog with her eye, and backed slowly out of his reach, found that every thing depended upon her ability to keep all her powers in steady action through what seemed an age.

We come to places where not only human lives, but the salvation of souls, may hinge upon our ability to hold ourselves to close, continuous attention. To look off for a moment means to fail utterly and lose the vital point. Well for us if our school mathematics, or some equivalent discipline has taught us to hold our thought in a given line.

There is an analogy between physical and mental hygiene. The body is kept healthy and its vigor increased by proper food as well as due exercise. It is impossible for the muscle to be firm and reliable unless the aliment is strong and nutritious. Neither can the mind be vigorous if it is fed on trash.

The racer in the Olympic games held himself to the closest diet during his preparatory drill. We are in training for mental and spiritual contests, upon the result of which are hinged the interests of eternity. "For we wrestle not against flesh and blood, but against principalities, against powers, against the rulers of the darkness of this world, against spiritual wickedness in high places." We must avoid all mental food that can impair our powers, for not the olive wreath nor the applause of the excited multitude will reward our success, but a crown of glory and the "Well done" of God.

What shall be our *mental pabulum?* Certainly not the cheap hash of events that is chopped up for us and sensationally seasoned by reporters and daily editors. If we desire to learn the art of forgetting, and surely the years will teach us that, let us cram our minds with what we have no wish to carry twenty-four hours. If we go through the reports of scandal suits, murders, domestic embroglios, and the like, it will be well for us if we are able to forget the bulk of what we read. There can be very little food for the mind in tons of such material.

Foul air, decaying vegetables, and diseased meats fatten for the maw of the pestilence the unwashed masses that fester in the alleys and dens of great cities. Dime novels and similar fulsome, sensual, vile publications poison the unthinking people, and fit them to be carried off by the pest winds of Mormonism, Spiritism, free-lovism, diabolism.

We will find healthy mental food in history, art, science, poetry and, above all, as a staple, in God's Book, that fountain and aggregate of all truth. We may indulge now then and in a little of the best-made fictional sweetmeats, but our minds can gain solid strength only from solid aliment.

We will not grow strong by devouring books. Seneca said, "Read much, but read few books."

The mental exercises of some students are simply mnemonic. Their knowledge is cyclopædic—all in quotation points. Such people are exceedingly convenient to save the time of thinkers. They can give you what you need on demand, with no rummaging of books, but when they need to put forth a personal intellectual effort, they are as weak and helpless as children. We are always wondering why they do not amount to more, and we conclude that being able to rattle other men's words from the pen's point or tongue's tip, may make a clever quotationist, but never a strong, rich thinker.

We must digest what we eat if we would appropriate to ourselves its strength. So we must make what we read our own by taking it to pieces and absorbing its substance.

To get the best intellectual strength let us learn first *our own language*, as Lowell calls it—"that wonderful composite known as English, the best result of the confusion of tongues." It is the speech in which we pray and praise, make our bargains and win our friends. It is certainly of prime importance that we should know the use and meaning of its words and phrases and sentences, so that when we intend to say one thing we may not give utterance to quite another, that, though like what we would say, does not convey its actual meaning. How much bitterness and heart-burning, how many quarrels would have been saved if they whose vernacular is English had so learned their native tongue as to be able to speak it intelligibly, saying simply and only what they mean.

How much more thought we could get time for, if we were not so busy with trying to find the exact meaning of what others have written and said. How much more actual Christian achievement there would be if the talking folk gave us their meaning in plain, exact language.

It is difficult to understand English without a knowledge of the wise, motherly, old Latin and also of French and German, for we must know that "phonetic decay and dialectic regeneration," as Max Müller would say, have so changed the face of many of our words, that we can get their exact significance only by going back to their early home and associations.

Linguistic study not only disciplines to readiness, it enriches and ennobles our thought. As the fertility of Egypt depends upon the overflow of the Nile, and each inundation leaves an alluvial deposit, so every stream of new thought that flows over the mind leaves upon it something of its own richness and strength. Whether it be the copious, resonant Latin, the imaginative German, the dignified Spanish, the musical

Italian, the polished Greek, the poetic Hebrew, or that wonderful Sanskrit,—a language mastered adds to the intellectual volume.

And this is true also of an author. If he has the verdict of the thoughtful and far-seeing, it will pay to read carefully what he has taken pains to write. We must not read along skimmingly, page after page, hoping to come to an understanding with him, and get at his meaning after a while. Let us read word by word, line by line, sentence by sentence, till we are satisfied that we take in the substance of his thought as far as we are able to apprehend its force. A few pages plodded through in this laborious manner, and our fine thinker is conquered. He can but tell us what he means to say.

A certain reading of Dante's "Divina Commedia" will serve to illustrate this point. A trio of friends, resting in the woods, took up the work of the mighty Italian, and read it in an easy, sauntering way, after the day's merrymaking or study. They usually left the poor victims of Dante's punitive genius to boil, or broil, and dropped off to sleep in the midst of the infernal terrors, with a peaceful sense of having done their duty by *la crême de la crême* of polite literature. Neither dared say to the others "Dante is certainly stupid, in spite of the eulogiums of the critics, and Longfellow's translation is wretched English." After a while it occurred to them to *study* this poet of whom so many fine things had been written and said. Then they found that each line was replete with poetic power, each sentence held some figure of speech all aglow with the fire of genius. They learned wisdom from their foolish waste of opportunity.

If one would go easily through a study, he must master its axioms at the outset. My friend has been supposed to have special power over the scraggy mathematical quantities that are such a terror to ordinary students. The secret of her success cropped out one day when she told me that her mother never permitted her to learn a new rule or theorem in arithmetic or algebra, till she had wrought some of the examples, studying out for herself the principle which was involved, and making for her own understanding a formula.

She learned also from the same wise teacher that a few hours of extra time given to the first chapters of a book where its principles are being laid down, will save days of lumbering, crippled attempts to wade through its later problems. "It is the first step that counts" in more senses than one.

Our Hebrew professor holds us for hours upon the first paragraphs of the Bible. "Get those words perfectly," he says, as he picks them to pieces, one by one; "know them in all their relations, and you will have passed through the gate that admits you to this wonderful revelation of God." He tell us that when he was a student in the Vatican University in Rome, his father, spending a few days with him, noticed a fault in his general reading. His grandfather had given him a hundred ducats with which to buy books, and he was quite proud of his little library. His father observed, however, that during the fifteen minutes between lecture hours, he glanced over the pages of a half dozen books, and before he had selected one into which he might dip, the time was up, and he had to go back to his professor. When he came from the lecture room, his father told him that during the three years that he was to remain in the university he could be permitted to read nothing but Dante, Petrarch, Goethe, Shakespeare, and Milton, because, if he kept up his studies as he ought, he would have only these fragments of time for general reading. It would not do for him to lose half his time deciding what to read, and the other half in getting hold of the thread of the author's thought. The writers chosen have an idea in every sentence. Their works may be opened anywhere, and there is something directly under the eye well worth the reading. They ennoble our minds by holding before them the finest imagery, the sublimest soaring of imagination, or the most subtle analysis of human character.

There is a double lesson in this rule of the thoughtful father: What we read must be of the very best, that that gives a full, rounded idea in the fewest words, and so is most provocative of thought, and also that we must use to the best advantage the odds and ends of time. The ordinary way of getting rich is by saving the small sums—economy in little expenditures. To get much knowledge one must use the scraps of time. Any avocation usually makes a demand that covers the whole of one's time. If he does his work well he has only minutes left for reading. Now, the one who crowds up to a better place where he may have firmer standing-room, and a broader outlook, is the one who thinks so carefully through the details of his work that he can do it more rapidly, and so save a little time; then he uses every moment to push his ability toward that to which he aspires. In this way, to him that hath more is given.

Some excuse themselves from reading on the

score of their being pressed with care, driven by business. We notice, however, that those same overburdened people manage to wade through any amount of matter in the daily papers, with now and then a cheap story that takes hours for the working up of its wonderful matrimonial *dénouement*.

Wesley not only studied philosophy, Biblical criticism, and philology on horseback, but he wrote excellent works on those subjects. We might, any of us, find time for a great deal of good reading if we would use the hours that are spent in driving to market, going upon visits, riding to and from business. We see in the street-cars whole rows of women who are gossiping with eye or tongue upon the cut of children's sacques, the style of ladies' cloaks, etc., and tiers of men who are intrenched behind a hastily written and badly printed sheet engaged upon a more expensive order of gossip, and one not always as innocent; but only once in a dozen rides do we see one—excepting always the students who are driven to use this time to keep up with their classes—who is busy upon some work that will give scope and breadth and grasp of thought.

Perhaps at most one can give only minutes to reading. Then let him read the best. If he will study with Shakespeare the modes of thought and expression, and the life of those old Elizabethan days, he will find that he has a gallery of antiquated English art next door to his shop or office, sewing-room or kitchen. If he has only ten minutes to spare, instead of gossiping with a neighbor about some ephemeral excitement, some nine days' wonder, or with *tout le monde* through the daily press about some larger item of astonishment, he steps into his gallery, shuts out the work-a-day world, and laughs or cries with the mighty magician over his Portias, Desdemonas, and Hamlets. Somehow he finds an interpretation of many of the little events of life, lifting them out of the commonplace, and showing how they bear, like the minor points in the plot of a story or play, upon the tremendous whole of being.

Men and women of genius interpret us to ourselves. If we listen to them, we may find the grand harmony of which even the discords are a necessary part. They will certainly give us to see through the shallow pretenses of the strutting, small people, and we will learn to seek the grand, ultimate good, even though it be by the way of Gethsemane and Calvary. The revelations of genius supplement and emphasize those of the Book of God. They are the outlying fringes of the meanings of the Infinite. Though they must never supplant the divine teaching, they may help to an apprehension of its fullness of thought.

Our thinking, to be right, must be from the right motive. Much fine thinking is in the interest of selfishness, mammon, sin, and so is all wrong. It may move men mightily, but it is down the inclined plane toward perdition. Such thinkers may be gifted with

> "The art Napoleon
> Of wooing, winning, wielding, fettering, banding
> The hearts of millions till they move as one,"

yet they are doomed to ultimate defeat. God's purpose is the only power that moves to sure, final victory.

Emerson says, "Hitch your wagon to a star." We would say, rather, Bring your tiny purpose into harmony with Him who made and manages the stars, and you can not fail of right results.

That our thinking may be successful, as well as right and strong, we must consecrate our mental powers to God.

Some well-meaning people mistake at this point. They take the service of God as something that is required, and must be gone through, like working on the road, or doing military duty; or they regard it a somewhat unpleasant necessity, like carrying a life insurance, to guard against a possible exigency. They mean to escape hell and get to heaven, but they intend to have money, place, and power on the way.

Now, let them devote their mental ability to the service of Him who claims all, and they will find that the primal use of *consecrated thinking* is the working out of a clearly cut crystalline character.

Others, who recognize more fully the Lord's right to the best of the life, mistake in this: they regard religion as an affair of the emotions, and having very little to do with the intellect.

They watch their sensibilities as carefully as a physician notes the symptoms of his patient. They keep diaries in which they note just how they felt at such a time, and under such and such circumstances, as if the condition of the feelings were a sure exponent of the state of grace.

Conspicuous among those who live by sentiment rather than by faith (which is another name for religious common sense) are the old Romish saints and recluses, who regarded pious meditations and introspection the sum of religious duty. They kept that most subtle and variable and uncertain part of the nature, the emotional, forever under the microscope. No wonder that they grew morbid and erratic, seeing visions and dreaming dreams.

It would have saved a deal of trouble if they had given their logic a chance to straighten out their *spiritual kinks.* And there are not wanting among Protestants those who are quite as foolish. There are consecrated men and women who are ready to pray and praise indefinitely, and to do any thing that will give a good, active tone to their *feelings,* but who seem to think it cold and heartless to pay any attention to the spiritual use of the intellect. They believe as surely as do Romanists that ignorance is the mother of devotion. They *feel* their way through the adjustment of their relations to God and men instead of permitting their reason to bear a proper part in the work. They bring their emotions to the happiest condition, but leave their power to think upon the tremendous questions pertaining to the spiritual life all unused and weedy, like a fallow field. The result is a character, one-sided, weak, superstitious, bigoted, liable at any hour to be warped out of all form and comeliness by the archenemy, and always unfit for the heaviest, strongest work.

As soon as one has attained a completeness of consecration that sets him entirely at rest about his own spiritual condition, he begins to obey the leadings of the Holy Spirit in caring for the souls of others. And just here there is the *greatest need* of sure, steady thinking. No work is more worthy of the best intellectual vigor than the work of God. In any thing else we may better be mechanical and blundering than in this, the most vital.

In every department of God's work there is need of a re-enforcement of strong, sure thinking. Many a good cause suffers, and some perish, for the lack of good management. That sad utterance of the Savior sounds like a dirge above the wrecks of good enterprises that lie along the path of the years, "The children of this world are wiser in their generation than the children of light." Diplomatists, politicians, business men study directness, polish, nice address, every art that has power over mind, to help them carry out their schemes, while the Lord's workers blunder through their duties in any sort of way.

We need to think more carefully how to *lead others to the Savior.* We will learn more for that work in the study of human mind, than in all good books.

We must not stumble in upon people, regardless of their modes of thought and action. We can not force a way into their territory just where we please to demand entrance. Every one has beaten routes through his spiritual domain—the tramways over which he carries his exports and imports. We must strike into them with our artillery and supply-trains, if we would conquer him for God. Some people have faith-force enough to construct military roads wherever they choose to go, yet we can not help thinking that the same zeal would accomplish infinitely more if the laws of mind were regarded.

For instance, see how cautiously a man "approaches" you, if he wants to insure your life. No rhetorician was ever more careful to assure an audience of his good principle, good sense, and good-will. If he began and carried his work as abruptly and unbendingly as some Christians set about *leading* a soul to the Redeemer, he would die in the poor-house.

There is a world of unnecessary lumber blocking up the way to the cross. Penitents are dragged through it by the force of conviction and the faith of the Church. When they find themselves rejoicing within the "wicket gate," hardly one in ten can tell by what process he reached that point. How much better it would be if seekers of Christ's salvation could be so instructed in regard to the way of faith as to know the principles that underlie the new life, being shown them as they take the steps by which it is made possible for God to change their relation to himself. They would then be like sailors who know something about the managing of a ship before they go to sea. When the storms of temptation strike them, they would know how to keep steadily on their course.

The newly converted ought to be cared for a great deal more thoughtfully than they are under the present *régime*. They are usually left to themselves when their names are fairly on the Church record. They need more help than ever when they really set about establishing a new character, and begin to understand how much there is to overcome. The Church is exceedingly remiss in this matter.

As if one should gather up fifty or a hundred little orphans and range them in rows of cribs with a table well furnished with meats and vegetables before each, and then lock them in and go on his way, rejoicing over his wonderful orphan house, and the grand men and women that were to be the outgrowth of his scheme; the ordinary methods of caring for Christ's little ones are not much less absurd. No wonder that such numbers are weak and sickly, and so many die.

Suppose some Sabbath day one should succeed in getting a dozen drunkards to take the pledge; then he should leave them — making no effort to help them find employment, better associations, and decent homes. They may go back to their old haunts among the whisky stenches, and fight the devils single handed till they shall chance to hear again the eloquence that roused them to a sense of danger. A thousand wonders if every one of them is not back again in the ditch by Saturday night.

We ought to use our very best thought upon this work of helping to assured, established Christian life the "babes" of Christ's household. If we know one of them to be staggering under temptation, we ought to take up his case as we would a difficult problem, one upon which were pending tremendous issues. If need be, we should spend hours in close, prayerful study, measure his infirmities, his peculiarities; think how he could be reached, how held. Trusting the Savior's help, ten to one, we could get him again out of Satan's clutches. If, through our lack of care, he is permitted to go back to his sins, his state will be infinitely worse than at first, for he will take to himself seven other spirits more wicked than himself. Thought given to this work pays abundantly. Did not the salvation of souls cost Christ his life? Heaven is eternal growth and glory, hell a fathomless horror.

Family religion gives ample scope for the best thinking. Family piety is one of the most potent agencies for the perpetuity of the Christian Church, yet how little do good people understand and use its power. In many families religious instruction is left altogether to the Sunday-school teacher and the pastor. If, from force of habit, the parents take the duties that belong to the heads of families, recognizing God at the table, and worshiping him once or twice a day as a household, it is in such a mechanical, meaningless way, that it were better left undone. A long chapter with never a question or a word of explanation or illustration, and a longer prayer. Little feet fidget upon chair rounds till they are nervous enough to fly in spite of the most dignified propriety. Big boys and girls rebel. The father scolds and tightens the rein for awhile, and ends in letting them do as they please. The mother protests in a meek way, and comforts herself with a determination to ask prayers for them, and to get the minister to come and talk to them, hoping that they will be "converted this Winter." Oh, what blunders! The power of music untried, the teaching of Scriptural truth with note and anecdote—giving Hebrew eyes with which to see into this wonderful Hebrew Book, that alone contains the way of salvation—all warm, genial, earnest means of home grace unused, and the children growing up to vote "prayers" an unmitigated bore, and the Bible the most stupid of books—driven to hate the faith of their fathers by the cold, formal attempts at family worship. How unlike God's plan for home piety and instruction.

"Hear, O Israel: the Lord our God is one Lord: and thou shalt love the Lord thy God with all thine heart, and with all thy soul, and with all thy might. And these words, which I command thee this day, shall be in thine heart: and thou shalt teach them diligently unto thy children, and shalt talk of them when thou sittest in thine house, and when thou walkest by the way, and when thou liest down, and when thou risest up." Even with this divine injunction as a model, there is need of the closest, strongest thinking, if one would train his family to earnest religious life.

Sabbath-school workers need to bring to their most important work well-disciplined, consecrated thought. In our public-schools, teaching is studied most carefully. Hours are given each week by each teacher to learning the best methods of imparting instruction. It is not enough that one is thoroughly versed in the study, she must know the best way of drawing out the young mind, and bringing it to exercise its powers upon the text-book in hand. She must understand how, with object lessons, pictures, blackboards, to make truth simple and tangible.

Sabbath-school teaching has undergone a change for the better, and yet it is only the specialists, the pioneer thinkers, who bring the same acumen to this work that is so useful in the public-schools. Their modes, that seem so wonderful by contrast with the old, humdrum ways of Bible teaching, do not come from the intuitions of genius, nor from a religious ecstasy. The love of Christ constrains them to put forth effort, common sense holds them to close thought, and thus they work out the plans that make the world-wide changes in Sunday-school teaching, just as thinking wrought Robert Fulton's crude notions of steam navigation into the *Great Eastern*—a floating city. Any one who knows enough to be intrusted with the care of a school or a class may accomplish similar results if he will give time and earnest, prayerful study to this question: "How can I give my scholars the most Biblical truth in the least time?"

Of all people *Christian pastors* have the greatest need of strong, steady thinking. There is room for improvement in every department of their labor. Take the prayer-meeting, for instance. Its outer mechanism is generally left to adjust itself. The shallow and bold are often allowed to crowd out the talented and timid. The prayers may be as long and mechanical, the hymns as wretchedly sung and tedious, the exhortations as prosy and tiresome as dullness and formality could desire. One needs a good degree of piety to carry him safely through some Church prayer-meetings week after week.

The young and moderately religious, the very ones who most need such means of grace, will not go, and there is no use in scolding. The only thing is to set about making the meetings better. They can be made as attractive as a social gathering, if one will take pains to pray and think out a plan for their proper management. The people hunger for spiritual food. There will be no trouble about the attendance upon the social meetings of the Church, if they are conducted in a sensible manner, and with the presence and help of the Holy Spirit.

Some ministers run in deeply worn grooves, round and round, year in and year out, doing exactly as they did a quarter of a century ago, though mechanics, art, science, teaching, every thing is constantly advancing.

As one of many points in which Church management is a failure for lack of sure, definite thought and purpose, we can but notice the singing. It has been proved in these latter days that more truth can be sung into the hearts of the people than they will take from sermon or exhortation. Yet, with all its power for good, Church singing is often useless if not positively harmful. It is left to shamble along subject to the caprice or vanity of thoughtless, irreverent people. Worship is suspended while the choir sings. If its antics are not amusing, they are immeasurably tedious. And this is not because singers are more troublesome or less manageable than other people. They are quite like others in doing a thing as it pleases them, when they are left to choose their own mode.

To remedy this mischief random shots from the pulpit will hardly answer in place of well-matured plans, upon which kind, common sense can bring all parties to agree.

In selecting the officiary of the Church the most careful thought is necessary. It would be a saving of time and strength to think and plan a whole day over filling an important office, rather than to let the matter drift, and then have to manage an unruly incumbent, or piece out one that is inefficient.

Any Christian to whom the Lord has intrusted a responsibility in his work ought to think what is the most possible to be accomplished in that line, and how the best can be done for the cause he is set to serve. With his power to think consecrated to Christ, "leaning not to his own understanding," but trusting for divine guidance and wisdom, let him study his material and arrange and dispose of it to the best advantage, making the very most possible of every opportunity, be it small or great. Then having done all, let him trust for the blessing of God without which nothing can succeed.

Some who come to understand that their failure in Christian work is owing to a lack of consecrated thinking, hope for a better life some time, but they do not comprehend their own responsibility in the matter, and the need that they bring themselves to a broader efficiency. They wait for God to send upon them an immense passional force that shall bear them up to a higher plane, suddenly changing the life to what it ought to be. They forgot that all human character is hinged upon human effort, that God supplies the grace and demands that we use it, we determining by our choice the direction and the extent of the divine work. Otherwise, the Lord, and not we ourselves, would be responsible for our condition.

True Christian passivity is *intensely active*, and while we meet his requirement God never fails to do his part. When one chooses that all his life shall be used in Christ's service, he will find that God works in him to will and to do of his own good pleasure. He will prove ultimately that the powers he was at such pains to wrench from their old selfish bias and turn toward God are by the Divine Father developed to their best strength. The Savior makes infinitively more of him than he could make of himself; and thus is demonstrated that word of the Master, "He that will lose his life for my sake shall save it."

Each talent given into the Redeemer's hand is by his power and providence brought to its best polish and strength and put to the very best use.

The Lord of the service sees to it that no work done with a brave, single-eyed purpose for himself shall fail of result. His word must accomplish that whereunto he hath sent it.

The scattered thought may lie for a thousand years like the grains of wheat in the mummy's hand, yet if it has in it the vitality of God's truth, it must spring up when the hour comes for it to have light and warmth and room, bearing a plenteous harvest of good.

Let Christian thought be thoroughly cultured and completely consecrated to the divine service, and the time will not be far distant when the Church shall move forth, "bright as the sun, fair as the moon, and terrible as an army with banners."

Then will dawn the golden day of peace, when

> "The last man shall stand God-conquered,
> With his face to heaven upturned."

MARRIED PEOPLE.

CONSECRATED thinking may yet master all problems of destiny.

Thought has already wrought marvels in the material world. Phenomena that used to set men shivering and cowering because they were believed to be the work of demons, have been found to be only the result of natural law.

In the older, more ignorant days, if an eclipse darkened the sun, or a tornado slipped its leash, or an earthquake moved forth in deadly might, the scared people imagined that dragons were devouring the worlds.

In this braver time science springs into the path of ruin wrought by the cataclysm, gathers its facts, finds its law, and guards against its return.

In the thinker's laboratory has been wrought out the wondrous mechanism that whispers from continent to continent, that makes patient draft-horses of fire and flood, that thrusts famine and pestilence and war back to their dens. In that same laboratory, by God's blessing, must order and well-being be evolved from the moral chaos.

As the problem of bringing erratic physical forces into harmonious action has lost much of its ruggedness and difficulty, so the inscrutable ethical questions that have loomed so hopelessly in the path of all who have wrought for the world's bettering, are giving way before earnest thinking, patient toiling, and steady faith for divine aid.

Evils that seemed as inscrutable and inexorable as destiny, grinding to powder the heart and hope of millions, have been analyzed by philosophic thought. The mischievous principle has been discovered and its elimination made possible.

In reformatory, as well as in mechanical endeavor, thinkers have stumbled over the simplicity of the right formula.

The old Greeks, of whom Plotinus said, "They used to get out of their bodies to think," wrought their best upon the questions of moral renovation. They move our pity—those men of peerless intellect standing, as Dante saw them in his dream, "with calm, slow eyes" fixed on the unyielding problem. They failed always in their studies of art, letters, and law touching the moral and social life. They fumbled in vain for the mainspring of the regenerated civilization. It is revealed by Christianity alone. It is nothing more and nothing less than *honor and integrity in the homes of the people.*

Aristotle was within touch of the secret. He declared the family to be the type of the state, thus almost guessing its tremendous import. If the mighty Stagyrite had taken another step and taught that the purity of the family is the power of the state, if he had found the divine method of cleansing that fountain of social activities, making clean the homes of the race, and if his dicta had been accepted in morals, as in logic, the gloomiest, bloodiest pages of history would have been spared.

Pliny said there would be no state if there were no family; an utterance that touches like the flicker of a taper the dense darkness that enshrouded his magnificent Rome.

Wolsey says that Rome rose by the sanctity of the family life and fell when that sanctity was undermined.

In the purifying of the home sanctuary is found the solution of that problem of the ages— the bringing into right lines of the immense ethical forces that have run riot, working such hopeless, reckless ruin, such boundless wrong and outrage.

The family can not be pure unless it is permanent, and its permanence depends upon the permanence of marriage.

Christianity alone makes provision for the permanence of marriage, because of all religions it alone teaches the inherent dignity of humanity, and the sacredness of inalienable human rights.

Marriage is of God. Jehovah united the first pair. He put to sleep his masterpiece, the wonderful complex being he had made in his own image, and wakened them to the happiness of shared work and joy; as if he had made tangible the gentler and more enduring part of human nature, clothing it in separate flesh that it might stand forth helping and helped, bone of man's bones, life of his life.

In the writings of the great apostle we find an amplification of the divine idea. "He that loveth his wife loveth himself; for no man ever yet hated his own flesh, but nourisheth and cherisheth it, even as the Lord the Church."

The Gospel rule of domestic life is above criticism. "Husbands, love your wives even as Christ also loved the Church and gave himself for it. So ought men to love their wives as their own bodies. For this cause shall a man leave his father and mother and shall be joined unto his wife, and they two shall be one flesh.

Let every one of you in particular so love his wife even as himself, and the wife see that she reverence her husband."

In all lands where the Bible has little or no power, the permanence and purity of the home are hardly known. Wherever Jehovah's will is not recognized as law, the marriage tie is a mere financial adjustment; men and women join themselves to each other from impulse, and separate by caprice.

No doubt there is a constant infringement of the husband's claim to reverence and love. Probably he is cheated out of all those delicate, refining attentions that go to make the best of life—that that we live when the public eye is not upon us, and we are simply and only ourselves. Yet, as the condition of the woman is the more gross and appreciable exponent of the wrong, of that we usually speak.

Among pagans *the wife is bought and sold*— the slave of man's lust or of his greed. Men hold themselves above moral restraint, and regard women as existing simply for their service and comfort.

Among the Greeks and Romans, even when those peoples were at their best, the woman might not have a thought above her distaff. She was the true woman who waited only upon the pleasure of her lord, holding her love sacred to him, living or dead, as did Penelope while the vagrant Ulysses wandered, heart and foot, at his own sweet will.

Cæsar's wife must be above suspicion, though the private morals of that same Cæsar, "the foremost man of all the world," were too scandalous for record. A married woman must sacrifice herself in utter disconsolateness at her husband's death, though he had given a dozen other women a full share of his love.

Christianity alone gives a woman the right to demand *honor* for *honor*, purity for purity.

Only the religion of the Lord Jesus Christ places the woman, where Margaret Fuller said she must stand to give her hand with dignity, "fairly upon her feet." You look in vain among the golden thoughts of the "Divine Plato" for one syllable that helps a woman toward the starting-point that the Hebrew Bible gave her —"a helpmeet for man."

When Socrates was turning his steady eyes upon death, and giving forth some of the finest utterances that ever fell from his lips, in that supreme hour when his heart ought to have been most tender, he turned from his weeping wife with a contemptuous fling at the weakness and silliness of women.

Hebrew women towered like desert palms above those of the heathen nations by whom they were surrounded—Sarah, empress-like in her beauty and strength; Rachel, whose life was so pure it stood the test of a seven years' courtship, "and it seemed to Jacob but a few days for the love he had for her;" Miriam, who made the songs of her people while her brothers were getting its laws from God; Jael, who delivered her nation by killing the generalissimo of the enemy's forces; Deborah, who administered law and led armies; Esther, the beautiful diplomate, who saved her race from the impending doom. Solomon, that pioneer of Jewish *literati*, gives us the *Biblical model* of feminine character. The picture is drawn with Rembrandt strokes. Compare it with those in the Vedas and Shasters. They teach that a woman is inherently vile. She was so bad a man in some past state of existence that she has been born a woman as a punishment.

The books of all non-Christian writers abound in proverbs about the intrinsic and hopeless depravity of woman. The Hebrew philosopher shows his belief in the opposite. He speaks of the virtuous woman as if she were not only a possible idea, but an actual person. He sketches from life. She is industrious. "She seeketh wool and flax, and worketh willingly with her hands." "She riseth while it is yet night and giveth meat to her household, and a portion to her maidens."

She is a business woman. "She maketh fine linen and selleth it. She delivereth girdles to the merchant. She perceiveth that her merchandise is good."

She understands the laws that underlie the rise and fall of real estate, for "she considereth a field and buyeth it."

She is any thing but feeble-minded, for "strength and honor are her clothing."

She knows something and can tell it in a wise way, for "she openeth her mouth with wisdom, and in her tongue is the law of kindness."

She is benevolent. "She stretcheth out her hands to the poor; yea, she reacheth out her hands to the needy."

She cares personally for the comfort of a well-managed home. "She looketh well to the way of her household."

She has a happy family life. "Her children arise up and call her blessed; her husband, also, and he praiseth her."

Her piety is the crowning glory of her life. "Favor is deceitful, and beauty is vain, but the woman that feareth the Lord, she shall be praised."

The degenerate Judaism of Christ's time had swung far enough away from the divine ideal. Its rabbis said, "He is a fool that attempts the religious instruction of a woman;" and "Let the words of the law be burned rather than given to a woman."

PAUL, whose utterances on this subject have been wrested by the unlearned and unstable to the destruction of thousands of souls,—Paul gives an epitome of his belief in this sentence: "There is neither Jew nor Greek, there is neither bond nor free, there is neither male nor female; for ye are all one in Christ Jesus." When the Christian Church cuts down through gloss and prejudice to the core of the meaning of that utterance we may look for the millennium.

The retrograde Christianity of *the dark ages* shut woman out of the world of sober thought and earnest endeavor, making her a drudge, or, at her best estate, a dainty plaything, on account of whose personal charms daft wights should write wretched rhymes, or doughty knights break each other's skulls.

In the sixteenth century Francoise de Saintoigné attempted to establish primary schools for girls. She was hooted in the streets of Paris, and her father called in four doctors learned in the law to sit in solemn conclave upon her terrible heresy, and decide whether or not the misguided woman were possessed with devils, prompting her unheard of and dangerous scheme of teaching girls to read!

In the eighteenth century Dean Swift wrote his "Letter to a young lady on her marriage"— a piece of literature which was received without dissent as an excellent bit of advice to a young gentlewoman. He says "It is a little hard that not one gentlemen's daughter in a thousand should be brought to read or understand her own natural tongue. But it is no wonder when they are not so much as taught to spell in their childhood, nor can they ever attain to it in their whole lives. I know very well that those who are commonly called learned women have lost all manner of credit by their impertinent talkativeness. But there is an easy remedy for this if you once consider, after all the pains you may be at, you never can arrive in point of learning to the perfection of a school-boy. Your sex give more thought and application to be fools than to be wise and useful. When I reflect on this, I can not conceive you to be human creatures, but a certain sort of species hardly above a monkey, who has more diverting tricks than any of you, is an animal less mischievous and expensive, might, in time, be a tolerable critic in velvet and brocade, and for aught I know would equally become them."

Phidias said of his statue of Minerva, "Give it the light of the public square." In giving this question the light of the centuries we find that in no land or time in all this sorrowful world has there ever been hope or heart for women except as the religion of the Lord Jesus Christ has borne sway. Women never had and never can have a firmer, better friend than the Son of Mary. Of all systems of philosophic and religious thought none has given her the place accorded to her by *Protestant Christianity*. They who strike at the Church because some of its limitations are faulty and irksome, are like the Ancient Mariner who shot the albatross. They will bring down upon themselves a doom more bitter than death, that of the abominable old sensualisms.

The Bible is woman's Magna Charta, and it is worse than suicide for her to set aside its pure, high truths.

Marriage is a Biblical institution. The home is found only in Christian lands. Without Scriptural guards a woman's life is poor and petty and pitiful enough. The woman who has sufficient moral dignity to desire to be nobly and truly herself, and enough insight to see where the danger lies, must cherish Christianity as she would her own life—nay, her own soul.

While the permanence of marriage may be nullified by the degradation of women, it is attacked no less fatefully *from another quarter.*

Before the abolition of slavery a southern lady wrote: "We women of the South are merely the heads of harems." It was a fearful thing for slave-women to be at the mercy of the lust of their masters. It was a no less fearful thing for the civilization and the home that the masters were thus rendered liable to a development of the low, the sensual, the animal. Thoughtful, Christian people in the South saw with the utmost pain the danger to free institutions from this terrible maladjustment. Where the mischief was allowed to enter a household the harmony and confidence necessary to a happy home were at an end. It did not need the genius of a Fanny Kemble for a woman to understand the cheat of giving her whole self to a man, while he divided his love between a legal family and two or three others not recognized by law.

Thus servitude avenges itself. The very presence of a subject class leads to a most harmful development of character in those for whose comfort the lower are deprived of natural rights. As "mercy blesseth him that gives and him that takes," so domestic wrongs curse the doer as heavily as the immediate sufferer therefrom.

Pagan men have proved this by the utter loss of all the "small, sweet courtesies," the tender, beautiful, bracing home atmosphere from which a man goes forth to face the rough, bad world, inarmored, invulnerable as Achilles was when his mother dipped him in the Styx.

Whoever holds another from a God-given right is guilty, not only of a crime against his victim, he sins most egregiously *against himself.* If he uses the power given him in his own domestic circle to perpetrate an injury that he would by no means endure from another, his sin is suicidal. He may be as handsome as a Turk, as proud as a Spanish grandee, as gifted as Lord Byron, as superbly selfish as Napoleon, yet he is stabbing to the heart the purity of his manhood, the integrity of his moral nature, and rendering impossible the best that this life can give him, the permanence and excellence of marriage and a home.

The mischief wrought in domestic life by *pride and passion* does not stop with destroying the dignity of marriage. It is felt throughout the community and the state. The vanity and insolence developed by being allowed to lord it over others, can but result in civil and national broils, brawls, and wars. The man who is accustomed to have his way, whether it be reasonable or sottish, is not likely to have himself well in hand in a diplomatic encounter. A government in the hands of such statesmen is in danger of constant entanglements and embroglios. The man who does not respect the rights of those upon whom he can trample with impunity can not be trusted to legislate upon the destinies of thousands who are at his mercy. In proof of this turn to those pages of history that record the growth and decay of that magnificent Persia, of the Roman Empire, of the Saracenic domination, of the rich old East Indian civilization. Self-government is at the base of ability to govern others.

It was not a mere accident that the apostle enjoined domestic *purity and integrity* upon the men who were to hold office in the Church, overseeing her interests and shaping her polity. "A bishop then must be blameless, the husband of one wife, vigilant, sober, of good behavior, given to hospitality, apt to teach, not given to wine, no striker, not greedy of filthy lucre ; but patient, not a brawler, not covetous ; one that ruleth his own house, having his children in subjection with all gravity (for if a man know not how to rule his own house, how shall he take care of the Church of God)." Before he can rule others he must learn to hold a tight rein upon his own passions. They who are accustomed, in little matters, and when free from outside restraint, to respect fully the individuality and all personal rights of others, can hardly fail of probity in public affairs.

Plenty of nonsense has been uttered and written upon the *equality and inequality* of the sexes. Probably a logical adjustment of this question is impossible, as it is based upon the comparison of things that may not be compared. As well may we attempt to measure mathematically the difference between color and sound, the fragrance of roses and the sheen of stars or other incompatible conditions.

If women reverence their husbands as the Scriptures enjoin, and men love their wives as Christ loved the Church, each will second the efforts of the other to make the most of any special gifts that may help the general good. The wife will not say, "It is for my personal comfort to have you devote yourself to money-making, so you must thrust aside that artistic or intellectual or benevolent ability that seems to dominate your character. You must not write or paint or preach as you believe you ought to do. You must make money to keep me and my children in ease and elegance."

The result of a domestic council upon the case may bring out the fact that, while he has the soul of sensibility, the fervor of spirit that might make him abundantly helpful as a moral leader, he lacks the practical ability that gets one comfortably ready for pay-day—an ability that, for some wise purpose, she has in full measure. Then she will take the commissary department while he devotes himself to the work for which he was especially intended.

On the other hand, he will not say, "These buttons must be kept securely sewed on, though your poem be never written, though your book wither and die in your brain, your benevolent scheme never find opportunity or use. Ten thousand souls whom your voice ought to warn of the wrath to come may stumble on in darkness to death, rather than that my coffee should lack the amber clearness your talent might give it, or my dinner the epicurean relish that your abundant energy might plan for my comfort."

The true equality, that of the Golden Rule, is not so very difficult to attain when Christ's Gospel has a chance at the lives of men and women. Under that principle, marriage is to neither a sacrifice, but a girding of the surest strength.

The home will stand pure and strong and glorious, the very bulwark of the civilization and of godliness.

Marriage is usually necessary to roundness and completeness of character. Each life needs another to which it may be joined by an unbreakable bond supplementing its lack by adding the quality or grace in which it is deficient. The timid man or woman must be united to the courageous, the brusque to the gentle. Joined, they make a completed life, each doing the better work for the influence of the other, each working freely to the law of his or her being, each following the will of God and working to his purpose.

There may be those to whom it is given to remain single for the sake of special personal responsibility with which marriage could but interfere seriously, but there can hardly be a more harmful fallacy than that marriage is opposed to holiness, and that they who would be specially devoted to God's work must keep themselves aloof from its entanglements. The Romish Church has committed its religious services to an army of celibates. It, is, consequently a strong political and militant organization, but, in meeting the spiritual needs of its communicants, it is an utter failure. Better a thousand times that its host of ghostly old maids and bachelors follow the example of the monk Martin, when he gave the sweet little nun, Katie Von Bora, a legal right to fill with rest and sunshine the stronghold where he retreated when hard pressed by the outside conflict, teaching thus by example as well as by precept how to do that most godly thing, the making of a pure, noble home.

There are also widowed hearts whose love lies in the dust of the sepulcher, and who adjust themselves to their loss as one does who has parted with an arm. Possibly marriage bells never chimed for them, but their hearts know the rest that comes only from the joining of two lives that are "meant for each other."

Marriage adds to the moral strength, instead of lessening it, but that this may be so neither must claim dictatorship. Each must respect in the other the ultimate supremacy and responsibility of the soul's choice.

But how seldom do we see wrought out this divine ideal. How wretchedly have sin and selfishness wrenched out of all form and comeliness this good intention of the kind God; and what *worlds of mischief* grow out of the sad mistake!

Multitudes are fastened together for convenience or pride, by diplomacy or avarice, really living, as blunt old Dr. Clarke has it, in "legalized adultery."

Many others who seemed at first well mated have grown into such coldness toward each other, we can but conclude they would be glad to be free. We can almost tell the number of their married years by the distance between them—husband and wife. What a disappointment! Instead of the expected paradise, only a desert of indifference! They are obliged to speak across this waste, arranging monetary matters. Now and then they catch a glimps of each other as they kneel side by side in the worship of God. The Lord winds the love of little children around their hearts to draw them together. Their tears mingle beside dying beds. They clasp hands by little graves, where seems to be buried the heart of each. Yet, in spite of all, they drift further and further apart—he married to his business or his ambition; she, to her babies, her housekeeping, or society. All those kindly glances, those touches of hand and lip, those gentle, loving attentions that were to have been the dessert of each day's fare, are forgotten or laughed at as school-boy poetry, or, like faded flowers from coffin lids, they are sighed over in secret. The twain grow old and die, utter strangers to each other's real life, altogether unaware of the strength and happiness they have missed by not living and loving as married people ought to do.

But this negative, this starving, is not the *worst side* of the mischief. The positive danger is far greater. Satan is not slow to bring in a brood of lawless loves to poison and destroy the hungry heart. If the affections of one wander wickedly sometimes the other is to blame. One is careless of the domestic bond because the other is selfish or cold, heartless or hateful.

Great harm comes to the children who are born into such families. When the household loves are frost-bitten, no brown-stone elegance can supply the lack of heart-warmth. From those frigid mausoleums daughters hurry off to find elsewhere what they have missed at home, and sons are easily lured into the by-ways of Hell! The children of such families not unfrequently grow up in doubt of the possibility of home-happiness, and conclude to repeat their parents' blunder, and settle into domestic mummies—their only relief, a costly embalming!

Married people can ill afford to freeze each other and ruin their children by their bickerings. Each icicle that falls between them, like the dragons' teeth sown by Cadmus, will spring up a hateful, malignant spoiler. It is so much easier to indulge a captious, petulant spirit than to hold it in check. People neglect those little foxes, surliness, snappishness, fault-finding, till they have spoiled all the vines. Such parents may help their children to good social position. They may will them a few paltry dollars, but they rob them of what is worth more than millions, the kindliness, the sweet memories, the culturing influence of true home love.

Let us find *some of the reasons* why so many married people fail of happiness. In the outset we may note a fault in the preliminaries. Married life is held constantly before young people, not in its own plain, beautiful, common sense simplicity, but tricked out with all manner of moonshiny sentimentalisms, and unreal fancies. The subject of getting married makes the staple of their jests, the main part of their merriment. Their amusements are planned with this thought uppermost. Their confidences are largely made up of the telling of love affairs. Their books outside of the school-room teach little else. What was that your boy hid under his pillow? A love story. And little need is there of hiding that sort of literature these days when even Sunday-school libraries are full of it. What was your daughter crying over? The tribulations of a pair of unfortunate lovers, the course of whose *affaires du cœur* seemed running at the usual unsmooth rate. Some authors catalogued brilliant have written but little except how people may get married in spite of difficulties and obstacles.

Sculpture, painting, poetry, music, all have been pressed into the business of drawing young people toward the Eden of wedded life. By this glamour during a decade of the most susceptible young years, marriage is made to appear the *ne plus ultra* of existence. For each there is waiting somewhere an angel that has chanced to be clothed in human form, and the chief end of life is to find that seraphic being and bring about a right understanding. But when the congratulations are over, the cake eaten, the flowers faded, the every-day dress resumed, the newly-joined pair find themselves thrust back suddenly into a *sober, matter of fact world* where people have to eat and drink, pay rent and doctor's bills. The angel turns out to be a only good-looking young fellow, who will smoke horrid cigars with his feet on the backs of the parlor chairs, and talk slang and pick his teeth at the table; or a pleasant little woman in a somewhat unbecoming morning dress, who has shocking headaches at inopportune times, and who cries to see her mamma when things are not exactly to her mind. "To work" is the verb that must be conjugated now in all its moods and tenses, though the mistaken pair expected to loiter sunnily through "to enjoy." If they had been held to better sense they would have found that the two are synonyms.

The fiction-steeped ambrosia and nectar begin to sour. The cream of life seems to be only bitter whey, and there they are, fast for a life-time, their happiness wrecked by a charming blunder!

That conviction, do you see, is as wrong as were their azure and gold expectations. They may swing back to a sensible view of the case, though some never do.

Young people ought to go through with their *courtship* with their eyes open. The blind Cupid is a pretty myth for the poets, but not one in whose hands we may risk our happiness for life. When a young man fancies that he is marrying perfection, we can but anticipate for him a disagreeable awaking. Knowing the tendency of human nature to extremes, we quite expect him to take a tilt in the opposite direction, and underrate the lady in the ratio of his present extravagance. That is what we always do when disappointed in any friend. We mark him as much too low as we had him before too high.

A little common sense is an immense help in such cases. Let the young man understand that his lady-love, though quite as angelic as it is proper for his wife to be, is simply human after all, made of about the same material as the mother who bothers him with her advice and worries because he does not heed it, or the sister whom he drives into the pouts now and then with his teasing. The same human stuff, only more thoroughly in his power—more easily hurt. His mother knows that he is growing away from her and presently he will go into a home of his own. His sister comforts herself with the hope that she will have somebody some day to love her boundlessly—some one who will not torment her so. But this woman knows that there is no proper way out of the reach of his burriness except to die.

Some set out with right notions, but they are quite too *prodigal of each other's love* and patience. They seem to take it for granted that the supply is exhaustless. To be sure, it took a world of effort to bring the affair to its present delicious state, but, thank Providence, it is happily adjusted at last. After the knot is tied they may be as careless as they choose to be about those little attentions and politenesses of which they were so profuse a few months before. This is a radical mistake. It takes more care to hold than to win a love. If it be worth any thing, and you are certainly not so idiotic as to think it of no moment that the friend nearest you should care for you always tenderly, you ought to *plan deliberately* to keep alive the sentiment you have been so fortunate as to inspire.

The graduate is a failure who stops studying when he takes his diploma. The victorious general who does not keep connection with his base of supplies will soon find himself in no enviable position. The young Christian who congratulates himself that he has nothing to do but to sing and praise will soon find that he has little left over which to rejoice. So the man who thinks his courtship ends with the bridal "yes," or the woman who backslides into the slipshod and easy-going as soon as her husband is caught, is sure to wreck domestic happiness.

Married people must not expect to *think exactly alike* about every thing. Of course, each must be firm in matters of conscience, but in the non-essentials let each defer to the other's preference, as far as possible. There is no use in arguing. Let there be candor and the utmost respect for each other's opinions in the consideration of questions about which there is a difference. If an agreement seems impossible, let that controverted point be fenced about—unapproachable territory—like the Elis of the Greeks.

The one who has most patience and self-control will probably win in the long run.

There are those who loved each other genuinely at the outset who have suffered the cares of life to crowd them into coldness and indifference. If the eye of such a one rests upon this page, let me whisper that *there is hope.* It is never too late to mend. Your love may have been cut down by the frost so that it has hardly put forth a leaf for a dozen years; but the roots are alive, and with care the plant will spring up again. Let there be an explanation, an understanding, if practicable. Let each decide to begin anew to live as people ought, with the help of the good God. It will be no small undertaking—much harder than to have kept right from the first. Your habits are against you, and you are less mobile in character, but it can be done, and *it will pay.*

Perhaps the mutual regard has been so long buried, the ground above it tramped so hard by neglect and coldness and little asperities, that its very life is a matter of doubt. But remember you are bound together for all time. Not only your own but your children's happiness is at stake. Give the love the benefit of the doubt. Act toward each other as if all were right between you. Keep back every impatient look and word as carefully as if you were trying to secure some great favor of a stranger. Try the effect of the little attentions that drew you together at first—the confidences, the silent deferring to each other's taste. *Begin anew* your courtship. Before marriage you always had for each other a kind look, a smile, a word of welcome. Try it now. If one comes in whom it is to your interest to please, it does not matter how tired or worried you are, you can smooth your face and put on a smile. There is no human being whose deportment toward you can affect your life like the demeanor of the one to whom you are bound for weal or woe. Better a thousand times please that one by your kindly courtesy than all the world besides. Let the wife meet her husband at the door with a kiss when he comes home from his day's work. If she goes into his office or store or study, let him treat her with as much politeness as he would use toward a stranger, and not intimate that she is a great bother, only "around after money."

Let each give the other special attention at the table, as though there were none there, not even guests, who are more to be honored. It will not be long till the ice will give way, and the warm tide of early love will be again pulsating through hearts that had nearly lost hope. This must be done or the united life that might be a bond of surest strength, will prove to be like the robe steeped in the blood of Nessus—a ceaseless, deadly galling.

You were deceived in your choice? The probability is you are far *better mated* than you think; and if you were free, you would do about the same thing again. At any rate, your one chance is to make the best of the case as it is now. That coldness may be only a crust of reticence over a warm, quick heart. The peevishness may be merely the querulousness of hunger for which no one is so much to blame as yourself.

Well for society and the world if the well-meaning, frigid people could be induced to begin anew a cordial treatment of each other, and thus happiness be brought back to many an empty-hearted, lonely home.

Married people are altogether too chary of their *commendation* of each other's good acts. They can criticise and censure and wax eloquent over faults, delivering themselves of proverbs, with homilies attached, *ad infinitum;* but a right good, hearty word of praise—it would choke them, one might think.

And an immense, psychological blunder is

that, to be sure. We are oftener helped to humility by honest, straightforward approval of our efforts than by scolding and fault-finding. Some who carry the bravest face are at the despair point because they amount to so little, staggering under a burden of fancied incompetency, needing far more than any one ever dreams a little encouragement. Help them over that hard place, and they will have time and strength to think of being actually humble.

Some men are full of praise of their domestic establishments behind the back of their wives—the very ones who need the good word—while, in the presence of the disheartened *hausmütters*, you could hardly draw a syllable of appreciation from them with forceps.

In old times good people used to put on their Sunday clothes and kid gloves before they dared speak of their religious experience; and their *love for their friends* fared but little better. If one spoke of the love of God shed abroad in his heart by the Holy Spirit, it was regarded a sure sign that he was a hypocrite. No clearer mark of a reprobate than to believe your sins pardoned, and have a disposition to declare the joyful fact. In those old iron-clad days if a married pair indulged "before folks" in any sort of manifestations of regard, they were set down at once as people who quarrel when the eye of the dear public is off their behavior. So they trudged on, those old saints, at infinite pains to keep the fire shut in most carefully, while those who were dearer than life were freezing to death at their side.

Unfortunately, this frigid mode of life has not all passed away with knee-buckles and ruffled shirts. There are plenty of married people yet who walk icily side by side, till one bends over the other's dying bed. Then, when there is little use, the pent stream bursts forth. The wealth that was intended for all those cold, hungry years, is poured forth lavishly, and it is all too late!

Let us be wise in time. God never meant this life to be a desert utterly barren of all that is good and beautiful and refreshing and glad.

Finally, in this matter, "Whatsoever things are true, whatsoever things are honest, whatsoever things are just, whatsoever things are pure, whatsoever things are lovely, whatsoever things are of good report; if there be any virtue, and if there be any praise, think on these things."

A home where Christ abides is a little *remnant of Eden*. The benediction of God falls vertically upon its blessed inmates. It can but be a power in the evangelization of the race, an armory where God's soldiers are equipped. Let Christian homes be constructed by that wisdom that is "from above, that is first pure, then peaceable, gentle, and easy to be entreated, full of mercy and good fruits, without partiality, and without hypocrisy." Then "the fruit of righteousness" will be "sown in peace for them that make peace."

Let the Scriptural law of unselfish love and reverence, based as it is upon the inherent dignity of humanity, and the golden rule of giving precisely what each would wish to receive from the other—let this divine dictum be observed.

Then shall the home be, what God meant in its plan, the center and stronghold of the civilization, the very exponent and chief guard of Christianity. Children born in such gardens of good will escape the spiritual warping and maiming that now so often sends them forth into the work of the world hopelessly tyrannical or cringing, self-confident or discouraged, unable to touch the problems of the future that press alike upon the sympathies and energies of men and women.

By the *arithmetic of heaven*, while one may chase a thousand, two can put ten thousand to flight,—the uniting of strength multiplying the efficiency by five. So of a good man and woman joining hands for the long walk through life, each free in Christ's freedom, each living by the divine will, and yet the twain united by the miracle of Him who honored with his presence the wedding in Cana of Galilee, and who must always himself unite the truly married,— the union after this manner can but increase infinitely the ability for noble work.

> "Two heads in council; two beside the hearth;
> Two in the tangled business of the world;
> Two in the liberal offices of life;
> Two plummets dropped for one to sound the abyss
> Of science and the secrets of the mind.
> In the long years liker must they grow,
> The man be more of woman, she of man.
> He gain in moral height, nor lose
> The wrestling thews that throw the world.
> She, mental breadth, nor fail in childward care
> Till at the last she set herself to him
> Like perfect music unto noblest words;
> Then comes the statelier Eden back to man,
> Then reign the world's great bridals chaste and calm,
> Then springs the crowning race of human kind."

SAVING THE LIFE.

THE Scriptures always sketch from life. They do not group figures for artistic effect, throwing awkward facts into the background. If their pages had been dictated by human wisdom, the immoralities of the patriarchs, David's sin, Solomon's defection and Peter's lie would have been left out, and so would the disputes of the disciples about which should be the greatest.

The Bible, like one who takes an instantaneous photographic view, brings before us people as they were, and not as they ought to have been. In this naturalness, this humanness, this truthfulness, may be found much of the force of its teachings.

The very defects of its characters are helpful, because they are so much like those that cripple us and deprive us of power for good. They are like signals of warning set up in dangerous ways, like light-houses built upon terrible rocks. They cry to us, "Beware, a great soul perished here!

Stand off, a nation struck that reef and went down!"

Probably none of the warnings of Scripture are more needed by many souls than that given in the *apostolic quarrel* about who should be the greatest. It was certainly a very weak and childish affair. A struggle for pre-eminence among the disciples of a Master who was so poor he had not where to lay his head, dependent for his food upon the charity of those who risked all in his service, and obliged to work a miracle to get money to pay his taxes. It was most inopportune. The gloom of Gethsemane and Calvary had begun to settle upon his soul. He was in the first act of the awful redemptive tragedy. It was unutterably discouraging. He was lifting to his lips the cup of doom prepared by sin for every human soul. He was about to taste death for every man. The life he was to purchase could come only by the casting out of the old, selfish nature. Yet those whom he had been teaching for three years, and who had been permitted to enter with him the very inner sanctuary of the divine presence, were giving way before the very first onslaught of the enemy, to that pride and selfishness that he was sacrificing his life to eradicate.

Foolish and inopportune and discouraging as

was that miserable dispute, it was no worse than what the Master has heard in the hearts and homes of Christians many and many a time nowadays, and always. That same wretched question echoes and re-echoes through our lives, day by day, like the ceaseless wash of waves.

The Savior was at infinite pains to bring them and us to a better understanding of life and its uses. He said again and again, "If any man desires to be first among you, the same shall be last of all and servant of all." Our stumbling so constantly at this point is a sure index that there is a *right impulse* of the soul, and a strong one, that has broken loose from restraint and lost its way, and from that comes the trouble. We desire to save the life from utter oblivion and forgetfulness.

> "To die,
> To sink as sinks the traveler who falls
> In the streets of busy London,
> When the crowds close in and all's forgotten."

This seems such a pitiful fate, so like never having existed, so like being blotted completely from the roll of being, we look about in desperate earnest to find something within the compass of our power that shall give us immortality. We want to clamber a little way above the common herd whose very names will be forgotten before their bodies fairly turn to dust. A fortune, political preferment, professional reputation, literary fame, something must help us to a niche in the rocks where we may write our little story with a hope that the waves may not wear it away for at least half a century.

Possibly we lack in genuine self-respect. We want to bolster our importance by some outward manifestations that indicate our consequence. We must distinguish ourselves in some way to set us at peace with ourselves.

Some have an inborn love of power, a deathless determination to stand first and foremost at all cost to others. The Alexanders, the Tamerlanes, the Attilas, the Cæsars, the Napoleons shine forth in the firmament of history, their lamps lighted at the altar fire, kept burning upon the shrine of godless ambition. They flame with a lurid gleam, like torches made ragged by the gloom, and flaring over pools of battle gore.

Like the attempts of the Egyptians to stave off the doom of forgetfulness by postponing the decay of the lifeless body, they succeed only in perpetuating the loathsomeness of death—their fame being little more than a disgusting mummy.

Jesus said, "Whosoever will save his life shall lose it; but whosoever will lose his life for my sake the same shall save it."

They who have really saved the life, living

through the ages in the continued vitality of their thought and action, are those who have wrought by the Master's rule, losing all in a single-eyed devotion to right principle.

Among the very first names upon this Roll of Honor, we find that of ABEL, the proto-martyr to the doctrine of justification by faith. His voice, muffled by distance, comes to us from the dim, early dawn, emphasizing the vital truth for which he died. "He being dead, yet speaketh," and his utterance is echoed by the most advanced religious thought of this, the latest century. "The just shall live by faith."

MOSES also saved his life by its loss. He found the greater part of the inhabitants of the globe segregated, nomadic. There were neither domestic nor civil institutions worth the name, because there were none based upon the eternal principles of right. Man as man had not enough inherent dignity to enable him to claim any consideration at the hand of another, except what muscular or monetary power could exact as his due.

Moses found the dominant race, the more highly civilized and intellectual, enslaving the the simpler and weaker, and keeping it under by murdering its children and forcing it to toil ceaselessly to fill the land with architectural marvels.

Impetuous in his fiery zeal, and full of enthusiasm for a grand principle, he threw himself into the work of reform. He slew an Egyptian who happened to be an exponent of the general oppression, and hid him in the sand. He found, to his cost, that he was working at the wrong end of the problem. The subject race must be made to comprehend its own dignity. The principle violated in human servitude is the inherent greatness of humanity, and they who are under can be trusted to rise to equality or superiority only as they apprehend this principle. Without that apprehension a change of position would be only a change of tyrannies.

To lift up a man or a race, one need not trouble himself to make the oppressor understand the worth of the slave. Let him teach the slave his own dignity, and trust him to make his master comprehend that lesson. The liberator must also see so plainly the tremendous import of human life, that he will go down among the oppressed and share the obloquy of their wrongs, sustained by his belief in the intrinsic human royalty.

To emancipate the degraded Israelites, Moses had to go to work, not as the Egyptian prince philosopher, the heir of the proud throne of the Pharaohs; he must count the wealth of achievement in lifting up the enslaved greater riches than the treasures of Egypt, with its affluent old civilization. It took forty silent, meditative years alone with Jehovah in Midian for him to learn that lesson. At last he promulgated his code, giving the wisest adjustment of the relations of men to men possible for many centuries. He epitomized common law, which, after the lapse of nearly four thousand years, wraps the civilized world in the mantle of its guardianship.

And what a grand saving of the life was his! To be able to lay a net-work of obligation upon all the races that recognize the inspired supremacy of conscience—giving to untold millions the happiness of a safe, protected life. What an expansion and intensifying of one's own vitality! What if he did wrap himself in a coarse Arab mantle and lie down to die upon Nebo, crownless, scepterless, throneless, with no shelter but the open sky, a houseless wanderer? For what better tent could we ask in which such a grand being should breathe out his life, than the star-gemmed heavens, with the sun in his strength and the moon in her brightness to guard his burial place—angels about him, and Jehovah to minister the last mortal rites?

ARISTOTLE was another of the glorious self-givers. It was his work to carry the world from the brazen into the silver age. Under his power, brawn yielded to brain. Muscle had been king and thought its slave. He reversed the order, and made the animal serve the intellectual. He taught the subjugation of the passions by the reason, and for twenty centuries his dictum has been obeyed in all the lands conquered by his genius.

He died in the outer, that he might save the true, strong, inner life. Of the Macedonian nobility, the tutor of Alexander the Great, endowed by his royal pupil with millions of money, covered with courtly honors, yet he held steady to the work in hand. No bribes could buy him; no flatteries seduce him; no successes inflate him; no glories swerve him from his course. When the tide turned, and the people for whose emancipation he had given his best years rejected his counsel and cast out his name as evil, he stood unmoved like a rock among the breakers, choosing rather to suffer affliction than to abandon the principles of right after which he had groped in his heathen twilight. He died an exile, yet the mighty reform he wrought in the domain of intellect has made reasoning reliable, and all emancipation possible.

The Greeks who lived and taught before Aristotle's day had a supreme contempt for humanity, seeing in it only the development of fine animal life, and regarding it of value only so far as it was physically faultless. Aristotle put his shoulder under the burden of the world's wrong judgment and consequent oppressions, and through all the long centuries the animal has never regained the ascendency. He died to all that was preferred by the people around him, yet he will live forever in the gratitude of the thoughtful.

MOHAMMED, also, gained all by losing all. He found the people groaning, almost unconsciously, under the beastly burdens laid upon them by their many gods. He tried to teach them a pure, monotheistic worship. They called him an impostor, and drove him from his native city. He persevered against all obstacles, till they came at last to believe that they had found in him their long-looked-for deliverer. Then came his coronation-day; and for four centuries the scholarship of the world was found among his followers. His life was a forfeit to his purpose to establish monotheism. He sacrificed to that work ease, pleasure, all earthly good. Only thus could he succeed.

WILLIAM, PRINCE OF ORANGE, enjoyed his broad estates and elegant life, probably, with a nebulous notion of human equality floating through his brain. In the midst of luxury, how could he know the hard life of the poor? In high favor with royalty, how could he understand the grinding taxation necessary to support regal pomp and glory? God meant him to be the champion of civil and religious liberty, and it took hard discipline to arouse him fully to the need of the hour.

The Romish Church stole his son, and that awakened him to a sense of its tyrannies. The Duke of Alva, with his dragonnades, trying to establish the Inquisition in Holland, made personal liberty a myth. When the silent statesman began actively to remonstrate, his estates were wrested from him; and then, with an empty purse, insufficient service, indifferent clothing, no place of safety, a price on his head, the proud Prince of Orange began to know the meaning of poverty. Then he became truly the friend of the poor.

When the great, hungry need of the oppressed people laid its hand upon his shoulder, he was young, rich, courted, full of the proudest, highest life. It led him, step by step, down the winding stair to its den of want. He became one with the common people. He gave all for their emancipation. When, under the assassin's steel, he was dying for their liberties, his last words attested the completeness of his identity with the cause of the poor, "O my God, have mercy upon my poor people!" A wail went to heaven from every home in Holland. He who had lost his life for the sake of a noble cause had gained the first place on his country's roll of honor and in the regard of all good men and true.

A man in our own country and time lived and died like William the Silent, losing his life for the oppressed, and saving it to the best and most enduring immortality. He gave liberty to as many millions as did the Prince of Orange, and humbled as proud an oligarchy.

LINCOLN came from among the "poor white trash" of the South, yet as princely a soul was housed in his rough *physique* as lived in the bosom of the man of elegant culture and noble blood. One has said of him, "His large palm never slipped from the poor man's hand. A child of the people, he was as accessible in the White House as he had been in the cabin. The griefs of the poor African were as sacred to him as were the claims of the opulent white man." Measuring all by their humanity, he found them essentially equal. Seeing in God the Father of all, he saw in every man a brother.

In the senatorial contest between Lincoln

and Douglas the latter was victorious. Lincoln said: "His life is all success, mine all failure. I would give every thing for his opportunity of working for the uplifting of the oppressed." After the hard discipline of the years, his hour came. He was found equal to the complete self-giving that marked him the Christly man of the ages, and in the achievement he gave all, holding steady to his purpose even when his friends turned from him in distrust. At last he gave his life for the cause he served.

He was like the century plant that we saw a few years ago. After seventy patient years it burst into glorious bloom, and then it died. After the supreme act of his life Lincoln went to God, and the mourning throughout all lands where liberty was loved was as if one were dead in every household. Said a Russian lady upon the shore of the Black Sea to a tourist, "So you are from America—Lincoln's land. When word came that they had killed him, I could do nothing for hours but walk the floor and say, 'Lincoln is dead! Lincoln is dead!'"

The Great Commoner, he interpreted to the people their own sense of dignity. Though he lost his life, he saved it by the suffrage of universal thoughtful humanity.

The life of JESUS THE CHRIST was the most

emphatic illustration of saving the life through its loss.

He who is "the blessed and only Potentate, who only hath immortality," "made himself of no reputation, took upon him the form of a servant, and was made in the likeness of men; and being found in form as a man, he humbled himself and became obedient to death, even the death of the cross."

He went down into the very depths of human lostness that he might put his great heart under the burden of the curse. Like a strong swimmer who had dived among the monsters in the caverns under the sea, he came up pale, exhausted, quivering in every nerve, but bearing in his arms a rescued race.

Of all who ever lived none so completely and abundantly saved his power for good, his vitality, his life as did Jesus. To-day the thought of the crucified Galilean is the mainspring of the civilizations. All bonds that bind together the nations and hold them back from savagery are of his weaving. All cords that draw them toward the throne of the Eternal are of his twining. He is not only the Way and the Truth, he is also the Life.

Since it appears plain that to make the life amount to the most in God's work, it is necessary to lose it, we may ask what it is to *lose the life* for Christ's sake.

Is it not to submit to his control all that goes to the make-up of the being?

Perhaps in no point of self-surrender does the will take a more stubborn stand than in submitting to him the conduct of the life.

Self-direction is the regal power. It is the crowning glory of human existence. Most thoughtful people will die rather than surrender to others this citadel. Thousands have preferred death to servitude, since nothing seems so degrading as unconditional submission to a human will.

It is not easy to surrender even to God the control of one's individuality.

It adds to the difficulty to know that for the sake of discipline and development He will probably lead us to just the work we most dislike, and hold us back from the things that we prefer.

A wise mother crowds out upon the playground the nervous, sensitive child that is forever poring over his books, while she holds to study the robust, roystering one who is always ready for any thing that will take him away from his lessons. So, in his efforts to bring us to completeness of character, God will probably have to lead us directly against our inclination.

If one is specially fond of public work he may be ordered to the rear, that in the retirement of private life his piety may be deepened, and his reflective faculties duly developed; while another who has thought and studied a great deal, shrinking always from public notice, may be sent to the front that he may be obliged to have new courage and daring, and because others need the result of his accumulated thought.

When called upon to place ourselves in God's hand we may have a premonition of this discipline that will make us draw back from the pain.

When the mother of James and John asked that her sons might sit, one on the right and the other on the left hand of the Master in his kingdom, he asked if they were able to drink of the cup that he was to drink of, and to be baptized with the baptism that he was baptized with. They answered "We are able." Probably they understood better the terms of promotion in the kingdom of the Redeemer, when the headsman's sword gleamed above the head of one, and the other was hunted from city to city by his persecuting kinsmen.

It may be helpful for us to glance at some of the specific points that come under this generic principle of self-surrender. Our wish *to acquire property* must be given to God. This is one of the first impulses shown by a little child. He pulls every thing toward himself, and cries if what he has seized is taken out of his hand. He must have every thing that catches his attention and pleases his fancy, whether it be his father's watch or the moon.

Nothing pleases the boy better than to have something for his very own, "to keep forever and ever."

When he gets older he sets himself to get the best of every thing. He may divide with the less fortunate, but it is because the name and sense of being generous may furnish more pleasure than the use of the trifle he gives—acquiring another gain, a finer and greater one.

After passing his thirtieth mile-stone he cares less for that pleasure and more for substantial acquisitions. So he begins to store away the dollars or their equivalent. He must have a place and stock of his own.

With most people of forty, fifty, and sixty, the determination to get property becomes the dominant purpose. They may flatter themselves that they do not love money, yet they hardly dare deny that they do care immensely for the consideration and the attention that the world gives those only who are accounted rich. It seems a fine thing to have elegant madames trail their costly silks in at one's door, while a coachman in livery drives the superb carriage up and down the street in front of the house, and to hear the rustle in an audience when one enters a church, or hall, and the sweet sibilants, "our first citizens," "our best families." Who would not enjoy the thousand and one obsequious attentions that are paid to the wealthy? Who would not shun the neglect, and coldness, and contempt with which the poor are usually treated. "The rich have many friends, but the poor is hated even of his own neighbor."

How often we hear the expression, "poor, but worthy," as if the terms were usually antithetic, and so must be separated by a disjunctive—the case named being an exception to the rule. That shows the general drift of the current of opinion, and few of us are of better mind, even though we be followers of the crucified Nazarene.

The spirit of the world is wrong in this estimate of people, and God means to set it right. If he gets us in hand he will spare no pains to correct our false notions. He will make us understand human equality. He will give us to see that a few thousands of money, more or less, make no sort of difference with one's intrinsic worth, and in order to that it may be necessary to give us a view from the lower side of the scale of his standard of values. Some one has said, "God shows how little he thinks of wealth by the class of people to whom he permits its possession." His nobility, they of whom the world was not worthy, "were stoned, were sawn asunder, were tempted, were slain with the sword; they wandered about in sheepskins, and goatskins, being destitute, afflicted, tormented."

The twelve, to whom the highest possible honor was promised, were driven from place to place with cruel mockings and scourgings, and all but one sealed their testimony with their blood.

Paul the noblest of them all, a prince of the realm, was familiar with hunger, and nakedness, and perils. He suffered the loss of all things for the excellency of the knowledge of Christ. While he sat in the dark at Damascus he was shown how great things he must suffer for the sake of the Gospel. And the Spirit showed him that every-where bonds and imprisonments awaited his coming. When we surrender to God this natural desire for the pleasant things of this life we are not at all sure but he may lead us to an apprehension of his estimate of human circumstances by some such processes.

If one is permitted to keep his property after accepting the divine will in the matter, he holds it no longer as his own, but always subject to the order of God. His sense of ownership is changed to a simple stewardship; so that, though he may not have to deed it away to a Church or charity, it is as certainly given up as if it had passed out of his hands. All this implies an immense overturn of natural tendencies, and the uprooting of habits that are the growth of years. No wonder it is called a crucifixion, and that it seems like an actual losing of the life.

Closely allied to our desire for property is our wish to be *well spoken of*—highly esteemed. This also must be surrendered. And in it, as in the other points of character that have been shaped by general opinion, we may expect discipline. They said of our Master, "He hath a devil;" and he says to us, "The disciple is not above his Lord."

It is no easy matter to consent to be led directly against the opinions of those to whose judgment we have been accustomed to defer. In that experience we begin to know something of the weight of the "cross of our Lord Jesus Christ by whom the world is crucified unto us and we unto the world."

The crucifixion of self-surrender would not be so hard if we could suffer one great pang, and have done with it; or if, in the submission, we might so lose our free agency as to be perfectly safe from ever drawing back unto perdition; or, if we could look our last upon the temptations of the world, and shut ourselves up in some sweet, quiet cloister, where there would be only prayers and meditations and holy offices. But it is the plan of God that we shall present our bodies a living sacrifice, and any drawing back will abate correspondingly our union with God, and our deadness to the world.

And just here we note one of the paradoxes of the Gospel. We are never so fully and completely alive as when we are dead. We have never so fully the symmetry of character, the strength, the enjoyment, the assurance of living by the law of our being, the certainty of success, as when we have surrendered all to the Master.

When we are dead, and our life is hid with Christ in God, we are most keenly alive to every worthy interest, we have the most glorious fullness of existence.

And what is *the life that we save* by the losing?

It is primarily the spiritual life, and it depends upon union with God. The original life of the soul was forfeited by sin. Grace finds us dead in trespasses and sins, and renews in us the life of God. We live this life more or less affluently in proportion to our submission to the divine will, and our trust in the atonement.

When, in the maturity of our Christian knowledge, we accept the will of Christ in all things, he will lead us not only to completed spiritual life; he will also give us the best physical and mental culture possible.

He will give us to understand that when *our bodies* belong to him, we must take care of them for him, and see that they subserve to their utmost the uses of the mind and spirit. We must give them good food, not to pamper false appetites, but to keep them in repair. They must have enough sleep, and only as much work as they can endure with safety. Well-meaning people have sometimes cheated God out of years of service by squandering their strength in overwork, or by crowding themselves through the drudgery of digesting the villainous compounds known as good fare, or by some other dissipation.

When we comprehend that our bodies are the temples of the Holy Ghost we will keep them clean as well as strong. We will not drink nor chew nor smoke poisons that not only hurt us, but make us offensive to others.

And it is doubted whether we will cut holes in our noses and ears for the hanging on of pieces of metal as the custom is in heathen countries.

We will stop our fretting when we come to know that the investment and use of our powers depend, not upon our puny wisdom, but upon unmistaking, divine judgment. We will cast our care on Him who careth for us: and with the care all taken off of the weak nerves, a little physical strength can be made to go a great way.

When our *mental powers* are taken completely out of the service of self and devoted simply and only to that of our Heavenly Father, we will comprehend not merely our privilege, but our duty to bring them to the greatest strength.

Satan crowds thoughtful people to study, that through their intellectual attainments they may gain money, refinement, luxuries, reputation, and friends. After grace has conquered their ambition, and they care no more for the pride of life, he holds them back by reminding them how much good has been done by people of low mental attainment. He would have them believe that it is better to give one's self wholly to devotion.

If God does not want consecrated thought to be developed in strength, why has he given us mental acumen above the simplest uses? Certainly the very best of every thing belongs to him, and nothing can transcend in polish or strength the needs of his work.

He wants pictures full of thought and feeling, so delicately traced and beautifully limned that they shall set us looking toward himself, the Source and Author of beauty. He wants poems as pure and strong as angels winging their way into the homes of the people, and singing God's truth into needy souls. He wants books, vital with his own thought. For this very purpose he has made artistic, poetic, and literary talent.

To be sure, some who have poor grammar, false rhetoric, and limping logic are used to win thousands to Christ; but who knows how much more might have been done by the same faith and fervor in a richly endowed and well-disciplined soul.

Never were so many persons converted under one sermon as under that of Peter, the Galilean fisherman, fresh from the Pentecostal baptism. Yet, afterward, that same Peter endangered the very life of the infant Church by truckling to Judaizing teachers. Paul had to withstand him to the face, because he was to be blamed. His undisciplined mind did not carry him through the task of settling the tenets of the new faith. It was Paul, trained in the best schools, who was used of God to give the Church its theology.

In the Anglican revival of the last century it was not the fiery eloquence of Whitefield, who came untrained from the common people, that organized the victory, but the quiet, steady, scholastic thought of Wesley and Clarke, with their broad erudition and profound culture.

We need not fear intellectual pride while we trust Christ to save us from sin. At all events, his salvation is our hope of immunity from that, as from every other wrong tendency. No amount of personal humiliation, penance, or mind-starving will have the effect to keep us humble in regard to mental ability. He alone is the deliverer from evil.

Above all, if we lose our life by surrendering it to God, we may claim and expect *the most thorough discipline* and complete development; possibly by processes not such as we would choose, but those that God sees best fitted to produce the result.

We will have to learn to be abased before it is safe for us to abound. It took eighteen years to bring Columbus to nerve and daring enough to enable him to discover America. John Bunyan preached like a son of thunder, his soul on fire with zeal for the salvation of the miserable masses. God permitted him to be shut up in Bedford jail for twelve long years. How his fiery spirit must have chafed! The world perishing, and he utterly powerless to help and save! But the result of that burying of energy was the production of his wonderful book, which has acquired an authority and circulation next only to the Book of God.

Wood fire must be pent, buried out of sight to make charcoal; and charcoal has to be shut in the very heart of the rock to crystallize into diamonds. So, when our life is given to God we may look for discipline that shall seem to shut us from the very opportunities we seek, but we will find ultimately that it was administered in the highest wisdom to bring us to a strength and fullness of life that will enable us to do the heavier, higher work.

> "Pain's furnace blast within me quivers;
>   God's breath upon the flame doth blow,
> And all my heart in anguish shivers,
>   And trembles at the fiery glow.
>   And yet I whisper, 'As God will,'
>   And in his hottest fire hold still.
>
> He comes, and lays my heart, all heated
>   On his hard anvil, minded so
> Into his own fair shape to beat it
>   With his great hammer, blow on blow,
>   And yet I whisper, 'As God will,'
>   And 'neath his heaviest blows hold still."

Our saved life will be hid with Christ in God. We will look out upon the petty squabblings and ambitions of the people as the mere bickerings of foolish little children.

As if the King had taken us into his palace and given us costly clothing from his own wardrobe, and all the fine, high fellowship of the regal life, we might look down upon the peasants at their sports upon the green with kindly, patient charity, remembering the days when we were among them, and as full of eagerness as any in the small emulations, the little strivings for superiority; but now their pastimes have no charm. We would only wish that we could win them to seek the royal favor, and trust the royal bounty till they, too, should become heirs of the kingdom, joint heirs with the Great Prince.

And what companionship would be ours— "with Christ!" what a secure hiding-place,— "in God!" Our "place of defense the munitions of rocks!" No care for the life that now is. Our "bread shall be given" us, our "waters shall be sure!" And for the eternal, the ceaseless life, our "eyes shall see the King in his beauty. We shall behold the land that is very far off!"

COURTEOUSNESS

POLISHED manners are not usually a passport to the confidence of good people, because flatterers and diplomatists depend mainly upon the soft address for their power to deceive.

The æsthetic has been the bond slave of evil passions, and the good have come to dread its potency. Fine culture has become effeminacy, weakness, voluptuousness. Forever in the historical rotations the cultured have become the degenerate and a prey to the rough and uncouth who are strong and virtuous.

Macedonian abstinence conquered Persian magnificence. Roman discipline mastered the elegant Greeks. The rugged Norsemen trampled down that polished Roman civilization.

Reading this the thoughtful have chosen the safety of rough virtue, instead of the weak polish of culture. The studied roughness of the Roundheads followed the profligate elegance of the cavaliers. Puritan angularities are a swinging to the opposite extreme in the purpose to escape the sensuous formalism of a corrupt, decaying Church.

Every one has seen enough of the evil doings of *especially smooth people* to make him suspicious of danger when there is in the manner a suggestion of *finesse.*

There are snaky people who can turn a corner as easily as can a viper. They wriggle into homes with their fine, obsequious airs, and charm every body with their polite attentions, their studious care of the good feeling of all. In the meantime, they are carrying out their deep-laid plans for self-aggrandizement, and secretly stinging to death all who are in their way. The honest, straightforward folk get so disgusted with these slimy, viperous methods, that they come to suspect an evil motive wherever there is a charming suavity. They swing to the opposite extreme, and prefer any sort of brusqueness to what they look upon as dangerous trickiness.

There are none whom we so dread as the completely selfish and unscrupulous Becky Sharps, and the crawling, detestable Uriah Heeps. Yet we do greatly err if we set down every expression of humility, and every kind, appreciative utterance to the score of a purpose to wheedle for selfish uses.

As the years clear our vision we come to understand that right and wrong lie back of the exterior. Chesterfieldian manners may gloss black intentions; and so may sanctimonious boorishness. Blandness of address is not of necessity a badge of badness.

It can not be denied that there are *false courtesies* that are used to win the regard for sheer, unmitigated selfishness. There are hypocrites who steal the livery of heaven to serve the devil in. There are chameleon-like people who change the color of their coat to suit the preference of the company into which they may chance to fall. There are the courtier-like—those who resemble the sycophants that dance attendance upon royalty, sunning themselves in its smile, and slinking away from its frown. Their baseness is proverbial. Indeed, the quality under consideration—courteousness—takes name from the same source that gives them theirs, hence, possibly, a little of the suspicion with which the sturdily honest receive people of fine manners.

There is, also, a supercilious counterfeit of courtesy that comes rather from a lack of apprehension of the intrinsic dignity of humanity, and of the law that regulates our relation to others, than from malignant selfishness. A man who could upon no account forget to touch his hat to a lady, and yet who can speak roughly to a pauper's child, knows nothing of true politeness. A woman may know by heart the rules of etiquette—the precise number of steps to advance or retire, the exact curve of the hand and bend of the head, for each salutation, and a faultless inflection for the pretty little nothings that society dictates for this, that, or the other occasion; and yet, if she speaks abruptly to her sewing-girl, sharply to her children, or peevishly to her husband, she has yet to learn the first principles of genuine courtesy.

The very fact of a counterfeit argues the existence of the real; and the free use of the spurious proves the possible power of the genuine.

There could be no hypocrites if there were no Christians to imitate; and the constant use of *finesse* demonstrates that abundant influence is secured by a pleasant address.

When one handles much coin he comes to know the counterfeit by the touch, the ring, the very color. Politeness that is from the heart comes to be generally known. It gives rest and warmth to the weary and heavy laden.

Heartless courtesies are like dead things, stirring with a galvanized mockery of life. The sensitive soul shrinks from them as we do from cold worms crawling upon the flesh.

True courtesy is born of self-respect and charity.

"Thou shalt love thy neighbor as thyself." The entire system of etiquette is epitomized in that sentence, and not the least important part of it is the last clause—*as thyself.* It presupposes appreciation of personal dignity.

No one who comprehends his relation to the Lord of glory, his possible coheirship with Christ to an "inheritance incorruptible and undefiled, and that fadeth not away," can be a cringing sycophant. No one with a sense of the dignity of redeemed humanity can be superciliously careless of the right to kind attention inherent in the very humblest and lowest. He can but understand that

> "Of one clay God made us all,
> And though men push and poke and paddle in 't
> (As children play at fashioning dirt pies)
> And call their fancies by the name of facts,
> Assuming difference, lordship, privilege,
> When all's plain dirt—they come back to it at last;
> The first grave-digger proves it with a spade
> And pats all even."

It is a nice thing to weigh one's own capabilities and adjust one's claim to respect. Some people are in a perpetual "claim quarrel" with society. Their demands are never met; and they are forever in a grumble—disappointed, unappreciated. Of necessity such fail to be courteous. They must first be reconciled to those about them who, as they say, have a pique at them, and then they can treat others with due civility.

Others undervalue themselves, though they differ widely from each other in their manner of showing their self-depreciation. They may blunder along through the proprieties, violating each principle, because they so constantly distrust their own judgment, fear to take their proper place, underrate their own dignity. In a perpetual purpose to get to the foot of the class, where, they seem to think, they are predestined to stand, they incommode the whole line, jostling a dozen others out of place. They make distressing efforts to be agreeable, but their shortcomings so confuse them that they are in a ceaseless flutter of apology. They never make up their minds to do a thing the best they can, and let that suffice—simply and plainly, if simple and plain has been their culture.

One who has sufficient insight to look down through outer glosses to the intrinsic worth, is never at a loss about his deportment. If he is taken into a circle to whose formulæ of etiquette he is a stranger he does not worry every body with his *apologetic nervousness.* He is simply and quietly himself. He does not compare his appearance with that of those about him, because he understands that the difference between social castes is very slight, at most. He sees that all are poor, weak humans together, each acting his *role* in the drama of probation, under his lidless eye whose judgment alone is final, and who notes, not the folds of the drapery, nor the pose of the head, but the thought, the spirit, the inner life. He knows that humanity is too great to be cramped down to the petty outside measurements that prevail among weak-headed snobs.

> "Is there for honest poverty
> That hangs his head, and a' that?
> The coward slave,—we pass him by,
> We dare be poor, for a' that!
> For a' that, and a' that,
> Our toils obscure, and a' that;
> The rank is but the guinea's stamp;
> The man 's the gowd for a' that.
>
> What tho' on hamely fare we dine,
> Wear hodden-grey, and a' that,
> Gie fools their silks, and knaves their wine,
> A man 's a man for a' that.
> For a' that, and a' that,
> Their tinsel show, and a' that;
> The honest man, tho' e'er sae poor,
> Is king o' men, for a' that.
>
> A prince can make a belted knight,
> A marquis, duke, and a' that;
> But an honest man 's aboon his might,
> Guid faith he mauna fa' that!
> For a' that, and a' that.
> Their dignities and a' that,

> The pith o' sense, and pride o' worth
> Are higher ranks than a' that.
>
> Then let us pray that come it may,
> As come it will, for a' that,
> That sense and worth o'er a' the earth
> May bear the gree, and a' that.
> For a' that, and a' that,
> It's coming yet, for a' that,
> That man to man the wide world o'er
> Shall brother be, for a' that."

Carlyle's description of *Burns's visit to Edinburgh* illustrates the genuine humility and manliness of the man who believed in the essential worth of manhood.

"This month he is a ruined peasant, his wages seven pounds a year, and these gone from him; next month he is in the blaze of rank and beauty, handing jeweled duchesses down to dinner, the cynosure of all eyes! We admire much the way in which Burns met all this. Tranquil, unastonished, not abashed, not inflated; neither awkwardness nor affectation, he feels that *he* there is the man Robert Burns; that 'the rank is but the guinea's stamp, that the celebrity is but the candle light which will show *what* man, not in the least make him a better or other man! Alas, it may readily, unless he look to it, make him a *worse* man, a wretched, inflated wind-bag, inflated till he *burst* and become a *dead* lion."

Why should we cower and cringe before those who may have had better food and clothing, higher-priced teachers, and more leisure than we? By God's standard our fare and our raiment, our lessons and wisdom may be by far the costliest and the best. The world's methods of measurement are all wrong. Let us learn to live by God's rule.

There have been various christenings of that *lack of independence* that makes plain people ill at ease in the presence of those who seem to be of more consequence. It is tenderly ycleped timidity, or bashfulness—*mauvaise honte* in honest French.

However it may be disguised, it is execrable, and betrays a weak character. The man who takes on the crawling order of conduct, not quite sure in certain society that he has a right to be in the world at all, is certainly deficient in self-respect. He is a coward, and that means that he would be a tyrant if he happened to get an upward tilt. Coward and tyrant are interchangeable terms, because both are based upon a wrong notion of the worth that inheres in a Christ-redeemed being, whether he be wrapped in calico or satin, in coarse muscle or fine, in abrupt manners or delicate address.

I know a man who sidles in and out of a

room to take up the less space, like Dickens's Mr. Chillip. He sits down in the most out of the way corner, tucks his feet under his chair, folds up his little frame like a pocket-lantern, and slips in his uncertain sentences with a wheedling simper, as though it was the height of superlative goodness that permits him to open his unworthy lips. It is impossible to draw from him a straightforward opinion even upon no more complicated a question than the state of the weather. He means to be truthful, but let one ask him if it is n't raining; "Why—yes—he guesses—to be sure—you know—well, it must be—it is," though a blink of sunshine through a blind that very minute contradicts his wriggling answer.

A dozen others who are not one whit more sure of themselves, don a brazen mask, and try to brace up by putting on independent airs. They are like the silly people who starve themselves in their thread-bare attempts at "keeping up appearances." They bluster, and stamp, and talk loud, and stalk through the room, lords of the manor surely! What do they care for rules? Etiquette, indeed! Superior to all such twaddle! After all their bravado they are not much unlike the scared little man who smirks in your face so provokingly.

I know another, of humble parentage and

narrow culture, a "working man," and withal a gentlemen. He is at home in any society because he is not ashamed to be his plain, excellent self, faultlessly polite, because dignifiedly self-forgetting and kind. He is no doubt innocently ignorant of some of the flourishes that pass for politeness with shoddy gentility, yet there is not a requirement of genuine courtesy that he does not understand intuitively, through his common sense, his self-respect, and his wish to make others happy.

Politeness is only a pleasant name for justice, and one can but be just if he has ample Christian charity. No one with the tender love of the Redeemer pulsating through his soul can be otherwise than kindly just.

This genuine courtesy is beautifully amplified in the thirteenth chapter of First Corinthians. The love that beareth all things, hopeth all things, endureth all things, does not flame up at every slight. It remembers that when one seems careless and negligent of the attentions that he ought to bestow, it is not impossible that a secret agony is gnawing his heart like the vulture at Prometheus's liver. It does not shy those who seem distant and indifferent. It gives them the benefit of the doubt, and determines, at all events, to keep its own temper generous and genial.

Ten to one its affability will win its way into the confidence and warmth of the most hopeless and unpromising reticence. Even churlishness will have to give way before its quiet radiance.

Courtesy belongs to civilization. Among savages its demands are met, in the main, if each lets his neighbor's scalp alone, and keeps his tomahawk out of the other's brain. As the social network grows complicated and interlaced, courtesy must keep pace with the need of intercourse, making it agreeable. It is of practical use in every-day life. Like the oil that lubricates the machinery, or the rubber pad upon the axle, it eases the jolts of the rough, hard-going circumstances that are posting us through the world.

Courtesy is like the spring check upon a brake, causing the train to stop by littles and not with a jerk that would send the passengers flying out of the windows or up through the roof. With due attention to the *suaviter in modo* one can use the *fortiter in re* with safety. It is the iron hand in the velvet glove that grasps firmly and without harm to the subject.

At best this is an out-of-joint world. All are burdened and weary. *Courtesy lightens the loads* and medicines the weariness. It is like fresh flowers, cooling drinks, and soft music in a sick-room. Though it may not have healing power in itself, it soothes the worn nerves, and prepares the way for more potent, remedial agents.

Much of our suffering is unreal. We are like children who shiver in the dark for fear of Indians that are beyond the Mississippi. We conjure up wraiths of possible trouble and have the gloom about us all a-mutter with dread may-happens.

A nervous man's note is protested a dozen times in his imagination when it is once really in danger. A fidgety woman's child falls into the river twenty times in her fancy, and she suffers all the agony of having him drown, except the certainty, while the little fellow is having a merry time at making mud pies on the bank. We suffer as certainly and sometimes as keenly from these unreal sorrows as if they were actual; and we need kindly patience and forbearance to stimulate and strengthen the mind to more healthful action. It is enough to drive one insane to be treated with abruptness and severity by some wise, coolheaded superior who sees the fallacy of the foreboding and is out of patience because we are so foolish.

When great griefs and bereavements come upon us and we stagger and grope through the loneliness of the empty rooms, the "small, sweet courtesies" make us forget for the moment

"The silence 'gainst which we dare not cry,
That aches around us like a strong disease and new."

We owe all people courteousness, be they black or white, base-born or high-bred, possible or real disciples of our Lord.

The flower lifting its bright face by the wayside owes me as much of beauty and fragrance as the Good Father has given me an order for, and the bird owes me a daily installment of heart-helping song. I owe every man, woman, and child with whom I have contact a word, a look, or a thought of kindness.

Many of the well-dressed, pleasant-faced people that we meet are carrying about "a lumpish, leaden, aching thing in place of a heart." Do we not owe them sweet charity? Do we go shouting and stamping through a hospital where men and women are lying with aching heads and throbbing nerves?

Christ teaches us to care for all who suffer, hence genuine Christians obey the apostolic injunction, "Be courteous," as certainly as they confess their sins and pray for pardon.

True courteousness is *an outgrowth of piety*. Said a sharp-eyed worldling of a professor of religion, "You can't make me believe that that man is a Christian. He is too rude; Christians have better manners." If there were no social ban upon boorishness, God's tender sympathies in the soul would make one courteous.

Nowhere is politeness more necessary than in the church, where gentle-souled Christians meet to worship the kind God.

I have seen a strange thing under the sun—strange and sad. A drunkard's wife, weary with the wretchedness and wrangling of her hut, has gone to God's house in vague hope of getting help to bear her burdens. Finding herself so shabby among the comfortable Christians, she has slipped into a pew, when a high-headed disciple of the crucified Galilean has driven her from the seat with a stony stare or a haughty gesture. Then there has echoed through my soul the cry from Calvary, "They know not what they do!" Better, a thousand times better, to go down into the sea with a millstone about the neck than to offend one of Christ's little ones.

I have seen a Magdalen upon whose heart had fallen the softening rain of God. As she went forth to seek a better life, she was met by a woman who drew aside to avoid contact with the penitent, and whose scourge of silent scorn turned the wretched feet again toward hell! The blood of that woman's baleful perishing could but rest upon the head of her *Christian* sister!

We must give to all kindly courtesy, for we may never know their sore need; but, above every thing, we must be courteous toward those who are *in our own homes*. Nowhere else is the lack of politeness, kindness, considerateness, so keenly felt.

Weary with the cares and worry of life, we rest in our homes, having laid by our armor; so it is easy to gall us with rough words and coarse, unkind acts.

Incivilities in the home are like sand in the eyes, and gravel in the shoes. No wonder they who have only sour looks and cross words where they ought to receive loving sympathy and care, are easily lured to destruction.

Some people treat casual acquaintances with more courtesy than they use toward their nearest friends. One-half of the incivilities they fling right and left, every hour, when free from the restraint of the public eye, if indulged elsewhere, would destroy every friendship they have outside the enduring home bond.

Savages sometimes tie an enemy to a tree as a target for bow and arrow practice; and yet there is a more cruel barbarism even in civilized homes. You may bind one to yourself with promises of lifelong love and cherishing, and then vent upon the luckless head your superfluous cruelty. By and by you will be unable to do your outside work, and you will need the rest and tenderness that are found nowhere this side heaven, except in a good home. Then the love that should have helped you bear the weariness and infirmities of age is scarred and withered and dead. No upbraidings, it is what it is on account of your own roughness and unkindness.

Some treat their *children* almost brutally, because the poor, helpless things are in their power. They forget that the harsh, cutting, bitter words that they throw around so recklessly, day by day, will be paid back, by and by, with compound interest. When one is old and crippled and broken, his children may do precisely as he did when he had the vigor, and they the helplessness. They will be respectful enough before folks, too proud to be caught using rudeness toward the decrepit old father; but when they are alone with him, if they have a touch of indigestion, or a business bother, then see how the hard, hateful words rattle about his helpless head. Does he recognize his own severe sayings of long years before? Whatsoever a man soweth, that shall he also reap.

Some parents love their children violently.

They will do any thing for them but restrain their own savage instincts; and so, unwittingly, they develop in them a harshness and hatefulness that will plant with thorns the path toward the sunset.

Children have rights that parents are bound to respect. They are as certainly entitled to courtesy and kindness as are parents. The injustices practiced upon them will be repaid by them when they come to power.

Who does not love to recall the pretty Quaker home in "Uncle Tom's Cabin," with the gentle mother directing the merry, young people with her kind, "Had n't thee better do so and so?" Where in this wide world is courtesy so beautiful or so useful as in the household?

Sometimes *brothers and sisters* are more ashamed of a caress than of a cross word. If they were caught hurling at each other a biting criticism, they would not be half as much embarrassed as they would over a kind commendation.

I was taking vocal music lessons once with a young lady of her brother. They were pleasant young people, and they thought enough of each other, yet I noticed that he used little incivilities toward her that would have finished my lessons at once if he had ventured to address me in the same manner. I said to him one day, after one of his usual sharp cuts at her dullness, "You don't like your sister as well as you do me?" He stared a moment. "Of course I do. I think enough of her. Why?" "Oh, nothing, only you never scold me when I make a blunder. You smooth it over very nicely; but if Lizzie sings wrong, you say so sharply, 'Now, what did you sing that way for? I've told you better than that more than a dozen times.'"

Many a girl whose brothers would do any thing and every thing for her happiness except treat her with the civility they are ready to use toward every other young lady, is driven into an unfortunate marriage hoping to find that respect and attention that we all prize so highly in the home.

And ten chances to one she fails in her matrimonial venture. There are men who visit every little *domestic mishap* and delinquency, the loss of a button, a rip in a glove, an accident to the morning paper, with an avalanche of sharp words as bitter and biting as a March hail-storm. Some put more gentleness into the voice when they address any living being whom it is to their interest to please, than they use in speaking to the wife of a dozen years. When the back of the dear public is turned they do not hesitate to practice toward her a thousand little abruptnesses, any one of which, before marriage, would have made a decided change in their relations.

Not every woman is so fortunate as the Scotch lassie who, standing before the minister with her laddie, declined to promise obedience. After two or three unsuccessful attempts to adjust the matter satisfactorily, the clergyman hesitated. "Ne'er mind," said Sandy; "I maun see to the 'obey' if there be strength i' this guid right arm." "Sae that's to be the tune," quoth the bonny lass; "weel, then, guid day," and she left him to seek a spouse that he could govern with less trouble.

Many a man who would scorn to lay the weight of a finger upon his wife in temper, shows upon small occasions of annoyance a petulance that hurts worse than a blow. Many a woman who is ready to sacrifice to the utmost for her husband's comfort, denies him the kindness of address and manner that she recognizes it her duty to bestow upon all besides.

Only at home, where courteousness is most needed, can it be properly learned. Let boys as well as girls be taught genuine politeness. There is no reason why "that boy" should be permitted to be a boor, while all pains are taken to make his sister a lady. If she needs gentleness and self-control for the work of life, so does he. The day is passing by when men are to be as coarse and rough as savages with a little awkward polish for court occasions, while women must be always obsequious and amiable. In the better time there will be no abatement of the best ideal of womanly self-sacrifice and meekness, and yet the *rôle* of angelhood will not be monopolized by her; it will be understood that it is also good for men to "be courteous," and to "be kind one to another, tender-hearted, forgiving one another, even as God for Christ's sake hath forgiven" them; "With all lowliness and meekness, with long suffering, forbearing one another in love."

Courtesy must be taught like music, beginning *as early as possible*. If you begin to teach your daughter music when she is nearly grown it will take a deal of practice to make her even a passable player. But let her tiptoe up to the piano and strike the keys as soon as she can stand alone, and she will grow up, other things being equal, its mistress.

If we would have our children courteous, we must begin with them early, and teach them by example as well as by dictation.

Gentle manners are beautiful, and there is always power in beauty. The touch of the sunbeam moves the granite column far more surely than does the wrench of the tornado. Harmonies of color, rhythm of movement, and melody of voice sway the soul with surer strength than can the force of reason or the grip of law. Let us be no longer afraid of what is beautiful because the children of this world, always wiser than the children of light, have prostituted it to base purposes. Let us conscript all beauty and elegance, and give it Christian baptism, and set it at work to help on the right.

Under the old typical law the firstlings and those without spot or blemish were used in sacrifice. Time will come when the best music need not be sought in the opera, the best art where it represents pagan or Christian idolatry, the best poetry in the service of Bacchus, Venus, or Mars. "The earth is Jehovah's, and the fullness thereof," and the day is dawning when the long arrears are to be collected.

The beautiful must be set free from its old associations, and, with the chrism of Christ upon its forehead, it must be wedded to the true and the good. Then may he who embodies all harmony and beauty and excellence reign over a regenerated realm.

MY NEIGHBOR.

WHEN the lawyer would test Christ's teaching upon moral obligation, he asked what he should do to inherit eternal life. The Savior responded by questioning him upon the "Mosaic Law." The question was quite in the lawyer's line, and in reply he epitomized the Jewish code in an able manner. He gathered in one statement all our duties to God, and in another our duties to our fellow beings.

He showed a fine analytic as well as synthetic power in stating, not the common frame-work of the duty, but its underlying principle. "Thou shalt *love the Lord thy God* with all thy heart and with all thy soul, and with all thy strength, and with all thy mind, and *thy neighbor as thyself.*"

We may imagine that the Master's keen eye was fastened upon the face of the comfortable, self-righteous lawyer, and the word slid from his lips touching like a lance of steel the core of the man's egotism, "This do and thou shalt live." Stung by an awakened conscience and "willing to justify himself," he asked a little petulantly, as we may suppose, "Who is my neighbor?"

The Savior, who always used consummate skill in dealing with human nature, did not answer directly. As a Jew he would have replied, "One of your race, or nation, or creed." As the Son of man he must give a broader scope to the obligation. But first he must, if possible, disarm the lawyer's prejudice, that the truth, which so clear a thinker was able to apprehend, might also be received into his heart and make him free. So the Master told a story, the dramatic interest of which would take the attention of the other from its personal point till the principle it was meant to illustrate had been accepted. It was about a Jew who fell among thieves and was neglected by the priest and the Levite—the representatives of religion and learning, and cared for by the Samaritan, a man of impure blood and corrupt creed. In conclusion the Master asked which was neighbor unto him that fell among the thieves? The lawyer occupied with the principle involved, gave a straightforward answer, "He that showed mercy on him." Then the lance of truth touched again his sordid soul, "Go and do thou likewise."

The lesson of *social obligation* taught in this parable may be formulated something in this way: The knowledge of need and the ability to meet it lay upon one a responsibility commensurate with his power to serve.

It is not optional with us to help those who need our aid. There is an obligation upon us as sacred and binding as it is possible for any to be, because it is one that grows out of the nature of our relation to others, and it is laid upon us by God himself.

Paul said, "I am a debtor both to the Greeks and to the barbarians, both to the wise and to the unwise." He has been much lauded for his generous self-giving, as if it were all gratuitous, unconstrained benevolence. He, however, with a clearer insight into the relation of men to men, regarded himself as simply discharging an obligation laid upon him by the knowledge of the danger of sinners and of their possible salvation made plain to him by the love of Christ which was shed abroad in his heart by the Holy Ghost. He says, "The love of Christ constraineth us." We suppose him to mean that he had been brought into such sympathy with the Redeemer's purpose to save all people that he had to live by the law of that love and knowledge, doing all that was possible to help every human being that he could reach. He is simply paying a debt that he owed to Greek and barbarian, bond and free. There was no merit in all those toils and travels, perils of waters and of robbers, shipwrecks and persecutions. He owed humanity that debt of service.

If he had been asked if this obligation was special, resting upon him and not upon others, he would have replied, *"No man* liveth to himself."

The warp and woof of *our indebtedness* are interwoven with the tissue of every other human life. None of us can cut himself loose from the rest and say, "I stand alone, owing no man aught." To every soul that needs our help, and that we may be able to aid, we are bound by a chain as unbreakable as that which holds the planets in their orbits.

We are debtors to our families, our communities, and the race.

We confess judgment when the first item of this claim is presented. Our very selfishness prompts us to care for *our own families.* If we neglect them, we know that we are planting thorns in the paths our feet must tread in the old years, when our steps are tottering and uncertain.

The recognition of our debt decreases in proportion to our distance from those to whom we owe service. It is like the rays of a lamp diverging and growing less in power with each yard of space they traverse.

The philanthropic radius is circumscribed with some good people, reaching hardly beyond their immediate vicinage. Their daily prayer, if freely translated, would be little more than,

> "Bless me and my wife,
> Son John and his wife,
> Us four
> And no more."

That we may bring our families to the broadest charity, the best life, the horizon of our sympathies must be widened.

Besides this home care we must recognize our debt of obligation to the *community*.

This caring only for those whom we can see and hear and touch, forgetting our obligation to all others, is a little as if one should pay his shoemaker promptly because he happens to live within sound of the man's hammer, ignoring the claims of all creditors who chance to live a few blocks away.

Some reach a little farther, taking in "our Church," "our town." Others have a sense of obligation that vitalizes those vague abstractions, "the government," "our country"—patriotism they call the sentiment.

If we search carefully enough we may find

the root of most of these benevolent impulses in selfishness. Unless our friends are respectaable and good, we are disgraced by their misdeeds. Unless our community has a reputation for morality, our real estate depreciates in value. Unless our country is prosperous, all our personal interests are in peril.

Only the few who have stood beside the all-loving Christ upon the mount of God can send their thought away east, west, north, and south to all races and tribes, peoples and kindreds, understanding that they are bound to all, no matter how uncouth in life, how rough in speech, how low in civilization, by the unbreakable bond of human brotherhood, Christian obligation. Only those divinely illuminated souls, looking away from that height of spiritual vision, acknowledge that they owe a debt of service to each wild Bedouin sweeping across his desert waste, each Esquimaux shivering in his snow-hut, each naked negro panting under the equator, each Indian *rajah* and Chinese cooly, each Siberian serf and American freedman, each drunkard staggering toward perdition, each lost woman hiding in her den of infamy, each vagabond child thrice orphaned and desolate.

Whether we apprehend the obligation or not, we owe a debt to *all our race*. None are so far beneath us but we can go down to their necessity; none so far above us but we can reach them to pay the debt.

All are in want. All suffer in their threefold life from its very beginning. Invisible harpies hover about the vestibule of being, and attack tooth and nail every little helpless human. The few who fight their way up through the multiform maladies of the first years, find themselves, even before Time claims his license to pull them to pieces, grievously hurt in all their triple life. It would puzzle the angels to find one who was sound even in body.

The whimsical, rickety, patched up old tenement is usually an exponent of the wretched life under its miserable roof. So the unsound body represents, not unfairly, the general pitiful mental condition. There are as few in complete health of mind as of body.

We use gentle names in speaking of *intellectual unsoundness*, for we do not relish awkward plainness in regard to our own ailments. We have "low spirits," "the blues," "hypochondria," when blunders, misjudgments, and evil surmisings indicate that the mental machinery is getting out of repair. When the disease has reached a given point, the general safety demands that the patient be shut within stone walls, subjected to careful sanitary treatment, and put in a strait-jacket.

We pity the poor wretches who have lost their reason as if it were an unusual calamity, yet we can not walk a block in any town without looking into the blank faces of fools who can not reason, the sharp faces of bigots who will not, and the close faces of knaves who dare not, use their reasoning powers.

Apish vanity, foxy cunning, wolfish cruelty, hyena-like jealousy, with all their kith and kin of brute passions and beastly appetites, lie in wait to mar and maim and poison the soul. You may wade through miles of people upon city pavements without finding one who is free from physical disease; so you may travel leagues without finding one unhurt in mind, perfectly sound in spirit.

Moral infirmities and maladies are even more common and pitiful than those of body or mind. Multitudes have felt the touch of the Great Physician, but very few of us have permitted him to bring us to even our own scant notions of moral health and vigor.

We dislike to look upon ulcers, goiter, idiocy, misshapements, physical and mental. If our eyes were opened to see our own moral deformities and those of the people about us, we should be driven to a hermit's cell to escape the painful sights of every day.

There is more tragedy in every life than was ever brought out upon the stage. Every feast has its skeleton. Under the peals of merriment and shouts of triumph may be heard the rattling menace of its fleshless fingers, the sullen chatter of its lipless teeth. Every human being, unless healed by the good Christ, is, by the witness of God, "full of wounds and bruises and putrefying sores;" and the worst hurts, the deepest gashes, are hid most secretly. They must be sought out, if one would help the sufferer.

You meet a man in society who looks robust enough to relish a good dinner and digest it satisfactorily. You exchange with him the commonplaces of the day, and then you go your way, like the priest and the Levite, leaving him in his utter darkness to stagger and grope and clutch after the rope of faith that has been wrenched from him by human treachery.

You are seated for an hour's talk with a lady. The worn pleasantries of chitchat are tossed back and forth gayly enough. If you would listen so wisely as to catch the hard whisper of her soul's dire need, the smile would fade from your eye, and the jest hurry back from your lip; for before you is not a merry-hearted woman, full of life and hope, but a wretched soul wrestling with fearful doubts of man's truth and God's pity.

Perhaps but little was required of you for the helping of these needy people. Only the cup of cold water. Not an exhortation nor a sermon, possibly not even an uttered prayer—only to give the bewildered soul a look into a pair of steady, kind, honest eyes, or the grasp of a clean hand—yet it might have held the wavering faith, till the courage had regained its strength. A world better if you had not been born, than for you to be delinquent in these simple debts—this throwing a rope to the shipwrecked.

A man is driving to market along a surf-beaten shore. In the last night's gloom ruffian winds and merciless waves seized a good ship and dragged her down to the cavernous depths. In the cold gray morning men and women are tossing in the breakers, clinging to spars and boards, and crying for help. What does our comfortable marketer do? Does he spring from his wagon and use every effort to get men, and ropes, and boats before the poor, drowning people are swallowed up by the hungry sea? Oh, no. He drives on, whistling a careless tune, and busying himself upon the probable gain from his load. What cares he for the perishing wretches?

Why, he does not know one of them even by name. He left his own safe in their homes. Lynch him? Not so fast. Execrable murderer as he is, he will live to a fair age if one who is without guilt must cast at him the first stone.

Victor Hugo in "*Les Miserables*" makes his bishop regard himself as having wronged the poor, because he bought comforts for himself with the money that he might have used in buying them bread, and Jean Valjean as no worse in stealing the articles than he in keeping their value from the starving.

The French philosopher may have overwrought a trifle his picture in his attempt to make us see our obligation to the poor, yet John Wesley was about as extravagant when he said, "If I die worth ten pounds men may call me a villain." Hugo's sad eyes have been fixed upon the maelstrom where the unfortunate are drawn down to death, unpitied and unhelped, till his brain may not be steady enough to work out the problem of their rescue; yet he lays a stout hand upon every man's shoulder, and with the peremptoriness of justice he charges him with unpaid indebtedness; worse, with the embezzlement of widow's crusts and pauper's rags. In the "cruel social juggle" he turns his sharp gaze this way and that for help, but in vain. Another, whose heart is no more deeply touched with a sense of wrong, but upon whose eyes God's light has been poured, may lead us directly to Christ, the embodiment of unselfish love, as the one cure of this terrible plague.

With the increase of knowledge comes an *increase of responsibility*. We are living in an earnest, restless time. Many "run to and fro, and knowledge is increased." Steam navigation, railroads, telegraphs have made all nations our next-door neighbors. The Celestial Empire has been towed across the sea and anchored to our Western coast. It is even emptying upon our country its surplus population. We have already in the United States two hundred thousand Chinamen.

It is an unambitious college that has not a Japanese name in its catalogue. One can hardly meet a parlor full of comfortably intelligent people without hearing one say, "I saw the like of that in Shanghai," and another, "We bought that in Calcutta."

The dark side of the world is rolling up toward the light. We adjust our postal and telegraphic glasses, and peer across the narrowing Pacific. We talk over at the breakfast-table what the East Indians were about last evening. Formerly those great lands full of queer people were all *terræ incognitæ*. The shreds of humanity packed away in them were so unlike ourselves in all their modes of life and thought, so far from our notions of what is essential to the species we hardly regarded them as human. But we have come to know that those immense masses of people, crowded and crushed together, as much alike as the individuals of a flock of blackbirds, and as meaningless in their jargons—mere census items, too numerous for counting—we have come at last to understand that they are hoping, fearing, loving, hating, sinning, sorrowing human souls, each redeemed by the blood of the Son of God, each capable of boundless development in good, each as dear to the Lord Christ as are the people by whose side we kneel at the home altar, or the communion rail.

We have come to know the *pitiful mistakes* of their civilization, how they grope for temple doors in their self-made darkness, and clutch each other's throats. We have seen how great souls among them, Confucius, and Zoroaster, and Mohammed, held aloft their flickering torches, only making the gloom more dense, while the people stumbled this way and that, sinking deeper into the mire at each step.

We have looked into their living places. We see them buying and selling their wives—their pride and passion trampling upon the very hearts of those whose love and care ought to make for them good homes. We hear the gurgle in the throats of the little daughters that they drown. We hear the moans of the old mothers pushed off into the Ganges, or left to the tender mercies of the wild beasts of the jungle. We know their misery. They have become our neighbors. We can not shake off the responsibility of sharing with them the light of our clearer day, the blessings of our Christian civilization.

Our obligation is increased also by the increase of *our ability*. Christianity is the mainspring of improvement in art, science, literature, civil and international polity; and with each added facility for commerce and travel there come new duties. Christianity and progress are synonymous. With the increase of Christian light there is added ability to bring things to pass, and with the increased power comes added responsibility for those less favored.

We can translate Bibles, and prepare and send teachers to the needy abroad as never before.

Instead of its taking months to make a copy of the Scriptures and months more for a sailing vessel to creep across the sea with its precious cargo, we can take the paper from the mill and the ink from the factory, and in a few days our ship has steamed around the world leaving at each port the Word of Life.

Fifty years ago it was a rare thing to find one who could read an Oriental language. Now, classes meet in our parlors hunting for Hebrew roots as an afternoon recreation, and our colleges turn out readers of Sanskrit by the dozen. It will not be long till a cued Chinaman or a nimble-witted Japanese professor will be teaching Oriental monosyllabics at each of our educational centers. Already in a national university in Japan is there a professorship of moral philosophy filled by a Christian missionary, who uses the New Testament as his text-book in ethics. If the sense of responsibility in the Christian Church had gone beyond that of the apostolic era in the ratio of added ability, long ere this the world would have been evangelized.

During *Paul's thirty-three itinerant years* Southwestern Asia and Southern Europe were dotted with churches. Not a city of consequence in the civilized world was left unvisited. Companies of men and women fished from the slums of heathen sensualism became the primitive Church, to whose purity and excellence we are never tired of referring.

When Paul was in Corinth, writing to the Church at Rome, he told them that he must carry to Jerusalem a benefaction for the poor Christians there from the Macedonians. After that journey he hoped to go to Spain and visit his Roman friends by the way. It was no small matter in those days of slow, unsafe sailing to go from one end of the Mediterranean to the other. It was as if one of us should write to a Church in Bombay, "I must carry a gift from the Bostonians to the poor saints at Athens. After I have performed that duty, I hope to go to Peking to preach the Gospel there, and I will stop and see you in Bombay on my journey thither."

If the sense of obligation to all men crowded the apostle to the Gentiles through all manner of perils and afflictions, how ought our added knowledge and ability to urge us onward in this work of the world's conquest for Christ. If the Church in these days were moved by that primitive zeal, every one of the dark-souled millions would have a knowledge of Christ's salvation within a decade.

In giving the ignorant masses, at home or abroad, *a knowledge of salvation* by Christ, we help them in all their hurt threefold life.

Christianity establishes not only Churches and Sabbath-schools, but it provides asylums for the infirm, hospitals for the sick, care for the aged, homes for the homeless, friends for the friendless, schools for the ignorant, health, peace, prosperity for all.

I might fill my house with the shivering poor, and it would become only what Christianity has taught every city and county to build—an almshouse or hospital. If I give those same poor people a knowledge of Christ's power to save from sensuality and vice, I make them self-supporting. Their sins are the one luxury that they can not afford. What they spend in intoxicants, physical and mental, would give them an independence, with ample medicine and care for their illnesses.

The religion of the Lord Jesus teaches us to crowd this common evangelism while we provide amply and generously for those who must be cared for by general public charity.

We can meet our obligation to our neighbors only by giving them a knowledge of Christ's power to make them pure and free, strong and noble. As the greater includes the less, this will be a medicine for all the ills that infest humanity, a lifting of the curse from our sorrowing race.

When we meet our ordinary financial obligations we take a receipt acknowledging the fact. We need *expect no credit* on this world's books for the expenditure of time and money and strength in paying the debts that we call benevolent. Indeed, so sadly are beliefs and notions of right jumbled, we will pass for fanatics and fools, if we do not spend our substance in adding to our own magnificence, rather than in bestowing upon others as God wills.

We can do this work properly only when we have reference to *the record above*, careless whether the eyes about us beam kindly or dart upon us scathing contempt and hate. The unslumbering Eye notes even the cup of cold water given in his name.

God never forgets. He will not pass lightly over any neglect of obligation. "My lord cardinal," said Anne of Austria to Richelieu, "God does not pay at the end of each week, but at the last *he pays.*"

He will hold us to the uttermost farthing if we fail of our duty to his poor, be they sufferers in estate or body, in mind or spirit. "Then shall the King say also unto them on the lefthand, Depart from me, ye cursed, into everlasting fire, prepared for the devil and his angels; for I was a-hungered, and ye gave me no meat: I was thirsty, and ye gave me no drink: I was a stranger, and ye took me not in: naked, and ye clothed me not: sick, and in prison, and ye visited me not. Then shall they also answer him, saying, Lord, when saw we thee a-hungered, or a-thirst, or a stranger, or naked, or sick, or in prison, and did not minister unto thee? Then shall he answer them, saying, Verily I say unto you, inasmuch as ye did it not to one of the least of these, ye did it not to me."

So wonderful is his condescension and tenderness of care, he will enter upon the Record and apportion the *eternal reward* as if each act of unselfish love and care of the miserable here had been done to himself. "Then shall the King say unto them on his right-hand, Come, ye blessed of my Father, inherit the kingdom prepared for you from the foundation of the world: for I was a-hungered, and ye gave me meat: I was thirsty, and ye gave me drink: I was a stranger, and ye took me in: naked, and ye clothed me: I was sick, and ye visited me: I was in prison, and ye came unto me. Then shall the righteous answer him, saying, Lord, when saw we thee a-hungered, and fed thee? or thirsty, and gave thee drink? When saw we thee a stranger, and took thee in? or naked, and clothed thee? or when saw we thee sick, or in prison, and came unto thee? And the King shall answer and say unto them, Verily I say unto you, inasmuch as ye have done it unto one of the least of these my brethren, ye have done it unto me."

Lowell's knight, in his vision, found this glorious truth—the same that the Master taught in the parable of the Good Samaritan:

"For Christ's sweet sake I beg an alms."

"Sir Launfal sees only the grewsome thing,
The leper lank as the rain-blanched bone,
That cowers beside him, a thing as lone
And white as the ice isles of Northern seas,
In the desolate horror of his disease.

And Sir Launfal said, 'I behold in thee
An image of Him who died on the tree.
Mild Mary's Son acknowledge me,
Behold through him I give to thee.'

Then the soul of the leper stood up in his eyes,
And looked at Sir Launfal, and straightway he
Remembered in what a haughtier guise
He had flung an alms to leprosie;
When he girt his young life up in gilded mail
And set forth in search of the Holy Grail.
The heart within him was ashes and dust;
He parted in twain his single crust,
He broke the ice on the streamlet's brink
And gave the leper to eat and drink.
'T was a moldy crust of coarse brown bread,
'T was water out of a wooden bowl,
Yet with fine wheaten bread was the leper fed,
And 't was red wine he drank with his thirsty soul.

As Sir Launfal mused with a downcast face,
A light shone round about the place;
The leper no longer crouched at his side
But stood before him glorified,
Shining and tall and fair and straight
As the pillar that stood by the Beautiful Gate;

Himself the gate whereby men can
Enter the temple of God in man.

His words were shed softer than leaves from the pine,
And they fell on Sir Launfal as snows on the brine,
Which mingle their softness and quiet in one
With the shaggy unrest they float down upon.
And the voice, that was calmer than silence, said;
' Lo it is I, be not afraid.
In many climes without avail
Thou hast spent thy life for the Holy Grail;
Behold, it is here, this cup which thou
Didst fill at the streamlet for Me but now;
This crust is my body broken for thee,
This water his blood that died on the tree;
The Holy Supper is kept indeed,
In whatso we share with another's need,
Not what we give, but what we share,
For the gift without the giver is bare.
Who gives himself, with his alms, feeds three,—
Himself, his hungering neighbor, and me.' "

HOW TO GET RID OF "THE BLUES."

FIRST let us acknowledge fairly that we are suffering from that horrid mental indisposition, and not go about with a machine-made smile and uplifted brows, trying to cheat ourselves into a belief that, though we are the most unfortunate and sadly abused persons on the planet, yet we are altogether saintly in patience—indeed, fair specimens of the noble army of martyrs. Let us lay aside our mask of wintery sunshine, and confess honestly and unflinchingly, "Yes; I'm in the blues. I know I ought to rejoice evermore, and in every thing give thanks, yet somehow my cares are quite too much for me."

Let us face the danger of indulging in the melancholy pleasure of being thoroughly wretched over every little piece of ill-fortune. Let us understand that, if we make mountains out of molehills of trouble, we shall abide under the shadow of snow-capped miseries all the long, long, weary days.

The diagnosis of the case will not be difficult if we apprehend the presence and importance of the disease.

There is a close analogy between physical and mental ailments.

Sometimes a part of the physical mechanism gets out of order, and the patient pays little attention, hoping to be well in a few days. The disease, meanwhile, creeps stealthily and steadily toward the stronghold of life, till some miserable morning the man awakes to the fact that he is at its mercy. It can be dislodged from the citadel of strength only by severe and energetic measures.

In like manner many a tired heart yields to a sense of discomfort that grows into a burden of care, an unbearable load, accompanied by all manner of forbodings, evil surmisings, misapprehensions, and heart-break, till the sufferer finds himself at last in a cell with padded walls.

Let us take these mental maladies in time; and first let us find the seat of the disease. There has been a deal of blundering at this point. Some of our wise moderns declare that a torpid liver is at the bottom of the mischief. They prescribe blue-pill or podophyllin to take the indigo out of affairs. They believe that the mental health hinges altogether upon physical conditions. Their one remedy for all the ills that flesh is heir to is found in good, generous care of the body.

They can not claim originality in these notions. The old Greeks put the highest premium upon physical and æsthetic culture as conducive to mental and moral excellence. They paid supreme national honors to the man of fleetest foot and firmest muscle. Their success in that line of development was unparalleled, yet they had a state of morals that could but give the gloomiest views of life here and hereafter. If they did not have "the blues" it was no credit to their common sense.

PLATO said: "While the soul is mingled with this mass of evil, our desires for truth can not be satisfied; for the body is a source of endless trouble to us, filling us with fears, fancies, idols, and every sort of folly. It prevents our ever having so much as a thought."

No one can deny that the body affects the mind, depressing it when out of repair and rendering it faithful service only when sound; yet we must insist that mental disease is usually out of the reach of physical remedies. From close observation, as well as from pitiful personal experiences, we may conclude that the mental disorder known as "the blues" is to be regarded simply as an aggravated attack of egotism, and as such it must be treated. Instead of saying, with amiable self-pity, "I have the blues to-day," let us use plain English, "I am suffering from an attack of egotism."

The victims of the disease are legion. The young girl at a party who is uncomfortable unless she has an opportunity to shine with special brilliancy at the piano or elsewhere; the young man who measures the enjoyment of the evening by the amount of attention he receives from host, hostess, or distinguished guests; the brother who has a good prayer-meeting only when he has the lion's share of the exercises; the woman who must lug into the conversation the story of the fine home she came from, the elegant people who are on her calling list, the trip to Europe she expects to take next year; the stupid old fellow who is forever telling of the things that happened when he was in college, the fine position his son is taking in business or political life, the excellent match his daughter is about to make,—each contented or wretched in proportion to the attention given by others to his weighty personalities—in cases like these the symptoms are so plain, there is little trouble with the diagnosis.

"But I'm sure I'm no egotist," says a reticent, sharp-browed man who carries an iceberg atmosphere about with him at least three hundred days of the year. "I seldom talk about myself or my doings. The fact is, I've felt a hundred times like shooting myself because I'm such a dunce."

You no egotist! Why, my friend, you have a determination to be first and foremost in all things, a purpose as inveterate as that that nerved Alexander to mow down human opponents as men cut grain. You have too much conscience to give the purpose full play, and because you have not brain enough to carry out your mighty egotism, you have a falling out with self. Every now and then you set your will as a flint to be somewhat in the world yet, and the failure leads you to the shooting point. Your egotism is ten times deeper and more dangerous than that of your braggadocio brother. His bubbles to the surface; yours seethes and burns like a pent volcano. Your reticence and disparagement of self are chains and rods that your conscience whispers necessary to keep the giant down.

"True, true," sighs a sad-faced Christian with a meek drawl of self-depreciation. "Egotism is a great hindrance to grace, and I'm thankful

I'm safe from that snare. I always feel to mourn over my own unworthiness."

And yet yours is one of the most inveterate cases of *spiritual* egotism—if there is such a thing. Half your moping over your narrow usefulness—as you cheat yourself to think it—is really dissatisfaction that you are not regarded specially successful in the work you attempt. If you will analyze the mortification over your failures, you will find that your grief is not usually because the Master's work is suffering loss, but because you yourself are likely to come out minus the *éclat* that is so very agreeable an incense to burn before the ego.

From observing these follies in ourselves and others, we have come to conclude that ordinarily the pain we suffer over hard circumstances, personal incompetence, lack of opportunity, possible, probable, and actual failure, which we call having the blues, is simply the result of more or less acute egotism, that can be gotten rid of only by remedies that go back of the physical, back even of the mental, and take hold of the spiritual life.

Webster defines *egotism* "a passionate love of self, leading a man to consider every thing as connected with his own person, and to prefer himself to every thing in the world."

Man has been sagely called a microcosm. This ridiculous passion makes every "little world" the center of the universe; as if each planet and satellite and speck of star dust should glance grandly around through the infinite spaces, and stretch its tiny rays to enlighten all, feeling its wonderful self the central point, the mainspring, the moving power of the whole; and then, if every planet, sun, and system did not in some way reflect its infinitesimal glory, it should fold in its rays as if it would mantle itself in gloom. Forsooth its efforts at shining are so utterly unappreciated that it may as well give up all attempts thereat, and punish the perverse indifference.

Egotism attacks us so *early*, we can not note its incipiency. We dawn upon ourselves so gradually, and so many of our earlier entries are written over, or rubbed from the record, we can not decipher the date of the birth of our self-consciousness. Richter is the only one I know who gives the when and where of his first cognizance of self—his discovery of the ego: *Ich bin ein ich*.

A little undue attention, an amount of indulgence that it is a pleasure to give, and almost immediately the child is brought under the power of egotism. Under the hot-house development process, all the pert sayings and pretty doings rehearsed before the helpless innocent while he is subjected to an infinity of adulations and flatteries, it will be strange if you do not see the self smirk in his eye almost as soon as he can go alone.

The little maiden sulking in the corner because she can not have the very finest doll her imagination can conceive, the small boy who is ready to burst into violent indignation because he can not whip every body of his size, and be acknowledged the prince and paragon in every mannish line—these baby humans are already in the advanced stages of the disease; and, ten chances to one, their very best friends by the sweetmeats given in mistaken tenderness have thrown them into the paroxysm.

Our school work is so planned that we run the risk of a strong development of egotism by our efforts to arouse children to a necessary mental effort. So perverse is humanity even in the dewy morning time, there seems to be only one way of getting the lumbering, clumsy intellectual machinery in motion—that is, by stirring up the egotism. "Emulation," minces the teacher; "Leaving off head," shout the children. All the same, a strengthened reiteration of the "Oh, how pretty!" of the nursery—a making of each child's consciousness the center of the universe.

Thus, in the cradle, through the school years and on, egotism is pampered and cultured. It grows with the growth, and strengthens with the strength, till its fibers become so interwoven with the very tissue of the being its removal is like cutting a tumor from a vital organ—almost equivalent to taking the life of the patient. In mature years not only do flatterers, who try to secure favors from us through our vanity, increase our opinion of our own importance, but our very efforts at self-improvement lead in the same direction.

Each human soul is a grand temple built by the Lord for his worship. Wonderful, ornate, glorious, but in ruins. Gates broken, avenues choked up, walls prostrate, arches fallen. When one looks into his own spirit, when he walks over the rubbish of wrecked powers, stumbling upon fragments of rarest architecture, bits of richest carving and gilding, jewels that might blaze in a seraph's crown, he can but feel the excellence of this masterpiece of God's handiwork. His language is a risky vehicle trundling over a rough causeway, fit only for baggage-trains laden with animal needs—he can bring no one into the shattered splendor. He can carry few specimens out. He can not explore the inner sanctuary of any other life. So he comes to think, though in ruins, his is *the temple, par excellence.* He tries to clear the avenues, set up the arches, polish the gems, and as he grows enthusiastic unless law checks his careless hand, he may wrench the guards from other lives, and tear them to pieces to build up his own. Thus did that prince of egotists, the great Napoleon.

Those diseases are *most to be dreaded* that skulk like an Indian enemy, or glide like serpents through the by-ways leading to the life. In egotism, as in consumption, the patient, up to the very last hour, clings to the hope that it is a mistake.

If you are sure you at least are exempt, set a guard over your thoughts for one-half day. See how carefully you hide any fact about yourself that is not altogether creditable. How ingeniously, and yet apparently without intention, you parade the items that reflect honor upon self. Your visit to the White House is sure to slip into the talk, while your sojourn in the backwoods cabin among your poor relatives never seems quite suited to point a moral, and adorn a tale.

How much more agreeable it is to have strangers regard you richer or better educated than you really are, than to have them make the opposite mistake. Not that you mean to deceive! Oh, no. But the habit of exalting self is so strong, you move in that direction without a noticeable volition.

If one touches yourself, how you resent the injury! He may strike at the selves of ten other people, and you can find a palliation for the offense.

If we detect in ourselves the symptoms of egotism, we will certainly desire a cure. Our very selfishness might prompt us to this; for not only does egotism make itself and all about unhappy by its exactions and discontent, it *defeats its own purpose*. This is illustrated by success in scholarship. As long as one is occupied with an earnest intention to get the surest knowledge of the theme in hand, he can but get on in his studies. But as soon as his success begins to attract attention and subject him to flatteries, he begins to fail, if he heeds them.

He is like a boy playing in the snow. He can make a straight line of steps as long as he keeps his eye on the goal; but when he looks at his own feet and notes every track, he makes a zigzag line in spite of himself.

The orator who is so full of his subject that he forgets every thing in trying to crowd upon his hearers the thought that stirs his own soul, is the one who is pronounced eloquent; while the one who forgets his subject in himself usually fails.

In no department of effort is egotism more surely fatal to success than in religious work. Those who have been specially used by God to carry forward his work are in great danger of this infirmity. Their good works come to be spoken of with praise; and they find it easy to lose sight of the fact that all reformatory power is vested in the Lord Jesus Christ, and their only hope of success is in humble reliance upon his working in them and with them.

When one forgets that he is only

> "A messenger at Christ's gateway
> Waiting for his command,"

he ceases to rely upon the Lord, and he soon finds himself shorn of strength.

He may keep up the forms of earnestness, he may use the tones and forms of expression that belonged to the time when he was full of power by the Spirit of the Lord, his talk may be full of stories of the old days when the pleasure of the Lord prospered in his hand, yet his effort comes to be like the mechanical movements of a corpse, loathsome and disgusting. His egotism has killed his usefulness; and unless there is a revivification, the sooner the dead is buried out of our sight the better.

Can egotism be cured? Can one who has become conscious that much of his thought is taken up with the interests of self, leaving but little vigor for high intellectual effort, or earnest spiritual work, one who finds his very humility a misnomer for self pity, his despondency over his failures simply a morbid craving for self-adulation—can such a one hope for a cure?

There can be but one answer. If one hopes to enter heaven, he must be saved from this infirmity—this sin. Otherwise he would not have peace even in the home of the glorified.

We who do not believe in purgatory must look for a cure in this life.

By what means can this be effected? Again, we find but one answer. Self-salvation is out of the question. We can not fortify self against self. It holds the inner fortress. The very pean of victory over its fall may herald its re-enthronement.

We can not reduce it to surrender by scourgings and starvation. Romanists have wrought upon that problem unsuccessfully for ages.

There can be nothing in the hour and article of death to work a radical change in the moral nature.

We must be liberated by a power not ourselves, above ourselves, in this life, or we must wear the chain forever.

Our only hope is in the word of the Master: "If the Son therefore shall make you free, ye shall be free indeed."

The salvation of the Lord Jesus Christ is the only cure for this inwrought, over-mastering selfishness. Unless the atonement itself is a failure—a tragical mistake, in Christ there must be an unfailing remedy for this and all other sins.

A reasonable command presupposes power to obey. God's injunctions are equivalent to promises. If we do our best to obey, he is pledged by his Word and held by consistency with his own declarations of purpose to give us needed grace and help.

Unless the commands, "Thou shalt love thy neighbor as thyself," "Rejoice evermore," "In every thing give thanks," be sheer nonsense, the power to yield complete obedience is promised in the all-sufficient grace of Christ.

There have been examples of men and women being completely cured of egotism by the power of grace, fiery souls that have become all tenderness and charity, turbulent spirits that have been changed into gentleness and patience; complaining, petulant egotists that have learned to give self utterly and joyfully for the salvation of others.

It was said of St. Jerome, "He subdued the wild beasts of the desert, but it took the Master of all to tame the lion, Jerome."

When we lay our selfish souls in the hands of the Great Physician for a cure, he gives us to know the meaning of those words of the apostle, "All things work together for good to them that love God." We rest from care of the adjustment of our relations and our work, for we cast all our care on him who careth for us. We are careful for nothing, but in every thing by prayer and supplication with thanksgiving we let our requests be made known unto God, and the peace of God which passeth all understanding shall keep our hearts and minds through Christ Jesus.

We will be able to say without hyperbole, "Thanks be unto God which *always* causeth us to triumph in Christ."

GETTING RICH.

WANT is universal. It tugs at every human heart. It sobs in the infant's wail. It echoes in the old man's moan. It jangles through our shouts of mirth. Its discords grate and grind in our songs of triumph.

The being that bears sway in this evil world is not the man of paradise with the chrism of God's "very good" upon his forehead. This man wants persistently, perpetually. He demands violently. He seizes furiously. A child in reason, a beast in appetite.

Yet he mistakes forever. He does not understand his own need. It is the mind that wants. It is the soul that starves. Will we never learn this? When we do, I think the millennium will not be very far away. This cry of want is ceaseless. It will not down. It is heard alike in cabin and cottage, hut and palace. Listen at the door of the heart of that savage. He gormandizes like an anaconda, and lies in the sun like a lizard. He cares for his mate and her young about as the lion does, sheds blood as ruthlessly as the tiger; yet through the beastly wrangling of passions, the low swash of the tide of brutish appetites, and the yell of cruel butchery sounds ever that moaning undertone of the better being,—hungry, hungry, hungry!

Turn to the man who sits a king. Not a king made of purple and gems, into whose hand has chanced to fall a scepter, but the one who rules in the thought realm, and makes laws for potentates. Listen to his secret heart-throbs. Is he satisfied? He, too, feels a pinching, wearing, perpetual want.

The present human state is abnormal. We are shipwrecked on an enemy's shore. Stunned, stupid, we can not decipher the cabalistic characters of the past. We do not know the vernacular of present events. We will not even bend our ear to the whispers of our own inner being. What wonders would be wrought by giving one half hour of each twenty-four to the study of self-needs. Listen to your own better life. It will tell you strange, new things. You have treated yourself as a nurse does the baby she doses out of the world. It moans—down with an opiate. It wails with hunger—thrust a sweetened, sickening compound down its throat. It writhes with pain—toss it, shake it, trot it, give it any thing, every thing but the patient attention, the sure care and healthful food for which it is dying.

Want prompts to acquire. A babe is hungry. It thrusts into its mouth its fist, or the corner of its cradle quilt, now a bit of broken pottery, then a flower pretty to look upon, but with a poison drop at its heart,—whatever comes within reach of the eager, senseless clutch. As aimlessly do grown-up children struggle to acquire.

One attempts to satisfy his hunger with epicurean luxuries. Dyspepsia and gout stand guard, but he will have these dainties for the animal, no matter about the consequence.

Another seeks elegant adornments. Worms from Europe, sheep from Asia, and small, wild creatures from Arctic deserts are put under tax. Human lives are woven and stitched into his fabrics, and yet he tires of their beauty. It can not quiet the inner clamor.

Another translates the cry into a demand for social preferment. He must rise above the common herd. So he tugs and toils, cuts furrows in his forehead, wears grooves in his heart, and scrambles upward. Yet the want, like the sea's eternal moan, surges ever through his life, only stronger for the aloneness of the altitude.

Another, a trifle wiser, thinks to purchase silence with choice mental viands. He seeks rare authors, books bubbling with the ripe, red wine of poesy, resonant with the grand, heroic chimes sounded down through the ages by noble souls,—yet never for an hour does the hunger cease its gnawings.

Most people think to satisfy themselves with *money* and the fine things it will purchase. Only fabulous misers who starve in garrets, bathing their leathery arms in golden coin, love money for its clink and glitter. The multitude seek it as the sinews of appetite, taste, and ambition. One has been trodden upon in his babyhood, chilled in his boyish years, his ragged coat jeered at on the play-ground. He sees that fine clothing brings gentle treatment and what passes for respect. He is cold and hungry. He must have gentleness and attention. They are in the market for gold. So he sets his purpose like a flint to get gold.

Another lacks courage. He rates himself at a low figure. If he can get the stamp of the world's mint upon his coinage he will believe it genuine. If he can have a good market price for his wares he will settle it that they are valuable. He will be satisfied, though he loses within an hour all they bring.

One has been robbed by death, and left quite alone, even in the chill morning gray. He fancies that money will buy friends, so he also gives himself to getting wealth.

We plume ourselves that we are not *ideal*—we are the plain, sensible people who say what we mean and believe what we say. Imaginative folk are they who gaze at the moon and make rhymes. Yet try us by placing a bit of paper in our hands with the national promise to pay in its criss-cross of engraved lines. It might mean to the monomaniac in the garret a thousand shining dollars. The sensualist clasps it in his eager palms and sees wine sparkling, cigar smoke wreathing, horses prancing, gems flashing, light feet tinkling, music rippling, laughter ringing.

To the artistic, it means a sail on the moonlit, castled Rhine, Swiss mountain views, studies of the old masters, rambles among ruins of Rome and Athens.

To the literary, it represents walks alone with calm-browed old sages, hymns of immortal vigor, racy chats with spicy moderns.

The dullest dolt holding it in his hand, the magic little possessive "mine" tingling on his tongue tip, would hardly fail to see in it the things for which he thinks the want within him clamoring.

We talk of the idealism of ancient pagans

who looked into the calm, mild eyes of the sacred ox to see the Spirit of Eternal Power and Patience—forgetting the beast in the idea for which it stood. We are not a whit less imaginative. We seize bits of green-tinted, pictured paper, to acquire which we have risen early and sat up late and eaten the bread of carefulness—we think we see in them the satisfying of the needs that crowd us to effort.

The ignorant Hindoo worships the image he carries in his robe. The Brahmin may claim to have his thought upon the spirit represented by the idol. Yet the soul of each is bowed before a low sensualism of his own production. The name matters little. The mode is of small consequence. If we were to demolish all the idols of heathendom, unless by some divine process we could get into the pagan soul a nobler idea of the Infinite, the result would be only a new harvest for the image-makers, a new growth of sensuality. To correct the disordered expression of our sense of need, the ideal must be renovated. The want must be interpreted aright.

Many of our *modes of getting rich* are honorable; but others are evil, even under the sanction of law. If a man chances to be born the heir of a coronet or a crown, that accident entitles him to the result of the hard work of scores of others who must starve, body and soul for his enrichment.

The trouble lies back of the grinding and oppression, the thefts and robberies. There is an unsound idea in the foundation of the social structure—a wrong rendering of the need—a determination to be rich in purse only, and not in mind and soul.

Under this *régime* three people have to be ground up, spirit and muscle, that the fourth may have the means of satisfying his hunger. The question turns upon who shall be the fortunate fourth in this struggle. The answer is usually the old formula of the survival of the fittest—the strongest of sinew or brain or will, or by that aggregate of will, known as law.

If they who have power to put others under tax comprehended that their own want could be satisfied only by the enduring riches, they would find means to live in the good and the right way, without harm to others.

We begin early to give our children a wrong bias in this matter. The want within sets the little one reaching after whatever is desirable. Parents, too thoughtless, too indolent, or too intent on getting money to give due attention even to so weighty a matter as the shaping of the characters of their children, satisfy themselves by flinging a legal barrier in the path of the inclination. There is no effort to teach the restless, grasping little being that it is a higher pleasure to give to make others happy, to share, to know.

He soon comes to believe that he must possess if he would enjoy; an error in the formulæ of the first chapter.

Then the tin savings-bank for hoarding pennies. To buy comforts for the sick child back in the alley, bread for the poor, Bibles for the heathen? Oh, no. To teach him to be saving. "To see how much he can get." Your child hardly needs to be taught that he must get and save money if he would be happy. The world will wear that lesson into him soon enough. Possibly as a birth-gift he has received quite too strong a tendency in that direction.

Mother, would you look for the ripened fruit of your careless sowing? See yourself thirty years hence, infirm, old, alone. Your son will not starve you in a garret. He is too proud for that—too humane, possibly—but not too humane to starve you in a corner of his mansion. He has grown rich. The soil of his heart is tramped down, trodden hard by the ceaseless round of bargains, sales, moneyed schemes. His life's horizon is narrowed, and its atmosphere has grown cold, till he has never for you a word of cheer or tenderness. He orders for you delicate food and expensive clothing, but he withholds the cup of cold water so sorely needed in your outworn life. Self-centered and sordid through greed of gain, he follows the bent you gave him when you had him under your hand.

We must make our children understand in the outset that to be happy is not to gratify every appetite like a mere animal, nor to strut about in showy plumage like a peacock, nor to keep upon the crest of the wave of excitement, forever amused and entertained; but, rather, joy is found in doing good, conquering self, making others glad, living by the Heavenly Father's law. Children can be taught these lessons. We have seen the experiment carried out successfully.

"Oh, yes," sighs an overtasked mother; "it is easy enough to toss off fine theories from a pen's point; but just step into my place once."

I know "mother" is a synonym for "sacrifice." I know there are mothers who stagger under the entire load of training the family—a load that is quite enough for two pairs of shoulders—while the senior partner of the firm gives himself altogether to the commissary department; but my exhortation is intended specially for those who make eating and drinking and appearing well the chief end of man. Better a thousand times leave the trimming off the dress and put the love into the heart.

When a boy is grown, he will be not a whit less a man for having worn garments minus ruffles and embroidery. He will be infinitely nobler if you spend the time carefully culturing the germs of thought and the growth of unselfish purpose. Now is your time. We reap in Autumn what we sow in Spring.

Novelists help on our foolish notions about getting rich. The old trick of having a chrysalis page or artist burst suddenly into a grand duke or prince is worn out, but the principle holds all the same. Hero and heroine must marry and be rich. Moral: Success equals wealth; wealth equals happiness.

Practical lesson: young man, get rich, honorably, if convenient, but at all events get rich. Young lady, marry a fortune; at all hazards catch a rich husband.

Society also helps strengthen this false order of things. Two friends meet. One inquires how a mutual acquaintance is getting along. These are sensible men. The question must refer to the growth and culture of the mind that is avowedly of prime importance. They are

Christians. It must look in the direction of the man's spiritual interests. Nothing of the kind. It means simply, How much money does he make. In what style does he live. "Oh, he is doing splendidly." How? Working out a plan for helping others into a better life? Turning many to righteousness? Growing in God's good will? No, indeed. Little cares he for moral distinctions or benefits. "Doing splendidly," in every-day Saxon, is simply getting money and spending it upon one's self.

The notions of society are miasmatic. Unless one carries a powerful disinfectant, he can but take in the poison. Only now and then one uses this precaution, so the majority take the fever of getting rich. That little adjective may mean a red flannel shirt and a string of glass beads, or it may mean a kingdom. It may stand for a big potato patch and an immeasurable supply of whisky, or it may represent an additional empire. Some fling society's "thus far" in her face, and take to the high seas with the prospect of being launched into perdition from the rope's end. Others cheat behind counters, more cowardly, but with no less risk of final loss. Some wait for gold to drop from dead hands; others plod on, year after year, to get rich by steady work.

We may flatter ourselves that we do not care for money. Possibly not, according to the aspirations of miserly A, epicurean B, or dashing young C; but it will be strange if our faces are not set towards some other point which means the same thing.

We are saying to ourselves, "Now, this sacrifice, this strain of will, nerve, or muscle, and then such a luxury, such style by and by." Here is a chaos of the odds and ends of desirable things which go to the make-up of a fortune, and which will satisfy no more when once acquired than do the cheap, simple purchases of to-day.

Nothing can be more hopeless than the attempt to satiate the soul's thirst with riches or the best that they can buy. They who have most money are the most eager to increase their wealth.

Some gentlemen in a public room in New York City were discussing the amount of property necessary to satisfy one completely. One man thought a quarter of a million would be enough. "No," said another, "I shall not leave business till I have at least half a million." "Pooh!" said a third, "one ought to have two or three millions."

Just then a money-king hurried into the

room—one of those who always go as if the hounds of starvation were snarling at their heels. With an apology for detaining him they asked how much he thought necessary to satisfy the desire for gain. "*A little more!*" he snapped, as he rushed on. His reply emphasized the fact that acquiring only whets the appetite to acquire. The acquisition of property does not secure happiness.

Fortunately very few reach the goal toward which so many tug and strain. And the few who call themselves "successful" are the most unsuccessful of all.

How seldom do you see *a rich old man* whose face is sweet, and calm, and restful. Most of them in seeking monetary wealth have neglected to acquire mental riches and spiritual affluence. See the ridges of care, the furrows of pain upon their foreheads, and the tense, sharp lines about their keen, uneasy eyes—lines of bitterness and disappointment. No need of prodigal sons and ungrateful daughters to plant with thorns their pillow of death. Long as is their rent-roll and profitable as are their stocks, they themselves are

"Heart-bare, heart-hungry, very poor."

Of all the calentures that lure to the grave, of all the *ignes fatui* that dance over death mires, none is so deadly as the greed of gain. Not alone is the body cheated out of rest and care in its treadmill, but the mind is robbed of development and the soul is wrecked eternally.

The Master, who never used words carelessly, said, "How hardly shall they that have riches enter the kingdom of heaven!"

We pity those who trudge ever in the service of toil, or slip on the icy stair of fortune, but how infinitely more do they deserve our commiseration who succeed in building for themselves a gilded mausoleum, a tomb not only for the burial of the poor outworn body but of the mind and soul.

> "Thus did a choking wanderer in the desert cry,
> 'O that Allah one prayer would grant before I die,
> That I might stand up to my knees in a cool lake,
> My burning tongue and parching throat in it to slake.'
> No lake he saw, and when they found him in the waste
> A bag of gems and gold lay just before his face.
> And his dead hand a paper, with this writing, grasped,
> 'Worthless was wealth, when dying for water, I gasped.'
> Be diadem or helmet on thy head,
> It must be arrow-pierced, and thou lie dead.
> Then every man whose mind is wisdom-stocked,
> Will strive to have his wealth in Heaven locked."

GIVING BY RULE.

THE world is in revolt, and God's main effort toward it is to bring about a surrender.

It is a principle of healthful reconstruction that each loyal subject shall use all his strength to bring the rest into subjection. God would conscript every thing in which there is power, and use it in the conquest of these revolted provinces.

If all who surrender to God would observe this obligation I doubt if the next century would dawn upon a single rebel. The trouble is, very few of us are in downright earnest to carry out God's plans.

We hire some one as economically as possible to offer eloquent prayers for us, and give us fine disquisitions upon morality; we give the pittance that is teased out of us by some one who denies himself almost the necessaries of life that he may make us see our duty toward the neglected masses, and then we settle back in our snug pews voting ourselves quite respectable, comfortable Christians.

God may collect arrears of us by force of arms. He obliged this republic, a few years since, to pay for cannon and ironclads what she would not give for school-houses, and churches.

If we will not evangelize the masses we must keep them under by armed force, and we find that God's police, civilization and Christianity, missionaries and Bibles, are by far the most economical, considered simply from a financial point of view. Riots and wars force men to give by the thousand in self-defense—men from whose grip a few dollars for God's work are wrenched most difficultly—and the moneyed outlay is by far the cheapest part of their giving.

Never before were there so many doors open as now to Christian effort. Red-handed war has torn open the rusty gates of sepulchral, old Eastern empires. China, Japan, India, Africa, South America, Mexico, with their swarming millions, are thirsting, dying for the truth of God. If the Christian Church, if Protestant America alone, would give and work as God wills, the world would be evangelized within the century.

Christianity is based upon self-giving. Christ is God's "unspeakable gift." They who are one with him in his work must go

> "Toiling up new Calvaries ever,
>   With the cross that turns not back."

He who is complete in Christ gives himself for the helping of others as certainly as did Jesus the Master, not as a propitiatory sacrifice, but as a working force. He may labor with his hands, as did Paul at Corinth; he may write dictionaries and French grammars, as did John Wesley; yet his one thought and purpose are to get all with whom he has contact, and whom he can reach with any sort of influence, back to their allegiance to God. And this is the normal Christian life. Any consecration less than this is unsound, unhealthy, defective.

When one has really given all to God's work it is unnecessary to argue the duty of giving money to carry on its operations. The greater includes the less. There is no use in prating about a "complete consecration" if one holds his dollars with a stingy grip, while the Lord's work is suffering for financial help.

It is a slender piety that lays by its wealth in diamonds and laces, elegant houses, handsome grounds, broad acres, bonds and mortgages, while the work of the world's evangelization is held back every-where for lack of money; laborers waiting to be sent to the whitened fields, those already at work recalled, schools closed, and men and women perishing in black ignorance by the thousand.

A few Christians give liberally. A smaller number *give methodically*. Before the Church meets fully its obligation in this regard every one who makes a public profession of faith in Christ must take upon himself a pledge to give by rule, and to the extent of his ability.

Nothing is well done that is not done by system—according to law. This holds in the simplest mechanical work. You can not make so much as a proper hoe handle without bringing it into right lines by the laws of mechanics.

We see this principle wrought out in monetary affairs. Two men start in business at the same time. One has a good capital and a fine opening for trade. He invests carelessly, deals recklessly, receives large return for some articles, loses heavily on others, and spends money freely, because he believes that his profits will warrant generous living. He wakes up some gloomy morning to find that his gay craft has been steadily a-leak, and his fine fortune is a wreck.

The other starts with a small capital, works it carefully, and by rule. He knows each Saturday night his approximate assets and liabilities, and guages his outlays by the figures in his ledger. After a few patient, plodding years he finds himself with a competence.

This need of living by rule is manifest, also, in hygiene. Suppose a child is fed once an hour or once in twenty-four, just as he can clamor somebody into attention, how would he thrive?

Suppose a man exercises one day till he drops from exhaustion, and lies motionless for a week, sleeps forty-eight hours, and then keeps awake till nature shuts his eyes by force, fasts a week and surfeits a fortnight, what do you imagine would be his physical condition?

Christianity has added fifteen years to the average of human life, and probably in no one hygienic point has it had the advantage more certainly than in its eating, sleeping, and working by rule. In all these matters its practice and methods are directly opposite to those of the savages.

Suppose education were carried on in a desultory fashion—a nibble of Greek, a browse of Latin or German as the inclination might be, mathematics or natural sciences to the taste, fact or fiction according to preference—what sort of scholars would we have with such a curriculum?

If I were sent outside of the Church for the raw material out of which a strong Christian was to be made, I should take the one who had been trained to live his physical and mental life by rule. He would have his strength well in hand, his energies under rein, where they could be available.

The Church should have all her force, talent, culture, money, general influence, where she could lay her hand upon them and make the very most of each item; and this can never be till each individual member learns to give as well as live by rule.

The very etymon of the word religion from the Latin *religare*, to bind anew, indicates the system to which its adherents are to be held.

Of all people Methodists are most at fault if they fail to work by rule. Some imagine that the grand religious awakening of the eighteenth century was a general riot of glorious irregularities. They could not be more mistaken. That freshet of Gospel truth that overflowed the massive, ivy-draped walls of the old Anglican church, and leaped John Calvin's iron barriers, obeyed law as certainly as do the planets in their orbits. They who wrought most wondrously in that mighty current were people who most positively slept and rose, talked and prayed, preached and wrote, lived and gave by rule.

Look at Wesley's prodigious methods. We think it wonderful for a machinist to hold an entire manufactory in his head—every wheel revolving, every hammer beating, every ounce of power weighed and adjusted in his tough, tireless brain. In Wesley's thought was the complex mechanism of bands, classes, societies, conferences, a membership of all castes, from Kingswood to the court; a ministry of all orders, lay, clerical, and episcopal. Think you his Herculean labors could have been wrought without the closest system?

We have a record of his beneficence. When his income was thirty pounds a year he lived on twenty-eight, and gave two. When it was sixty, he lived on twenty-eight and gave thirty-two. When it amounted to a hundred and twenty, he kept himself to the frugal twenty-eight and gave ninety-two. It is estimated that, from the proceeds of his publications and other sources of income, he gave in all over one hundred and fifty thousand dollars. His last entry in his benevolence account reads thus: "For upwards of eighty-six years I have kept my accounts exactly. I will not attempt it any longer, being satisfied with the continual conviction that I save all I can, and give all I can, that is, all I have."

God's idea of a ritual was given in minutiæ to the Jews. Their one temple was built under his direction, and it was a marvel of beauty from base to cap-stone. Its service was most expensive. In the very outset one twelfth of the people were set apart for teachers and priests. The other eleven-twelfths were to support them, relieving them from the necessity of laboring for their daily bread. It was distinctly specified that every Jew should give one-fifth of his income to the service of education and religion.

We believe every Christian ought to give at least one-tenth of his income to the work of God; one-half as much as the benevolence of the old dispensation.

This plan of giving a tenth to the Lord would be economical. Nine-tenths of our financial troubles grow out of a slipshod keeping of accounts. The large percentage of business ventures that result in failure is probably owing to the fact that many go a little beyond their ability, hoping that by some turn in the wheel they can meet their obligations and come through safe. A financial gale strikes the sea. The waves dash higher than they expected and the outcome is wreck and loss. If they had kept their accounts so that they could know at any hour just the condition of their finance, they could have prepared for the storm in time.

These careless business people never can tell exactly how they stand. They never know the precise appreciation or depreciation, of a piece of their property. They hope it is about so much, and they are apt to look at their belongings as people do when they eat cherries with magnifying glasses on so as to make them seem large.

Facts are relentless, however, and the bankruptcy that might have been spared if a plain, simple, sure reckoning had been taken, comes on apace. Women are accused of ruining their husbands by their extravagance, when, as the case often stands, it was the man's careless method with his accounts, making himself and his wife think themselves worth much more than they really were, that did the mischief.

If one promises God one-tenth of his income he can not be honest unless he knows all his receipts and expenditures that he may get at the exact amount due his benevolence account.

One ought in self-defense to give at least one-tenth of his income. Covetousness is a cardinal sin. One-twelfth of Christ's body-guard fell through covetousness. Christ was so poor he had not where to lay his head. The expenses of his itinerant tours were paid by women who risked all to follow him. He had to work a miracle to get a piece of coin for tribute money. Certainly the disciple of such a poverty-stricken teacher was in far less danger from love of gain than we who have houses and lands, stocks and bonds. It behooves us to walk carefully where an apostle fell.

Very few escape an attack of covetousness. Many who are liberal while they are poor, discover a thirst for gain as soon as they begin to acquire. In cholera times we use disinfectants. Systematic giving is God's guarantee against the miasmatic taint of avarice. Others as good as we have grown avaricious. Ten chances to one we will fall into the same snare unless we take special means for its prevention.

Those who have done the most for God's work have been among the most self-denying and systematic givers. Mary Fletcher, though a woman of fine tastes and culture, lived upon twenty-five dollars a year and gave the rest of her income.

Selina, Countess of Huntingdon, gave up her liveried servants and expensive equipages, selling even her jewels, and living in the simplest style that she might have the means to buy and build chapels for the poor, and to turn theaters into places of worship.

Dr. Coke gave to God's work two fortunes. Near the close of his life he arose in the British Conference and asked for the establishment of a mission in India. He was told there were neither men nor means for the work. He replied, "I have yet a small estate of one thousand pounds. I give that and myself with it to go to India. If you refuse my offer you will break my heart." I have read of an English Methodist who looks for divine direction in his business and gives by the Pauline rule, "as God prospers him." A journeyman mechanic, he set up a small business on borrowed capital. Eight years after he pledged to give fifty guineas a day as his missionary subscription. Eliza Garrett, of Chicago, to whose benevolence many of the Methodist ministers of the North-west are indebted for their theological education, the foundress of Garrett Biblical Institute, gave all her property for that work, reserving for herself only two hundred dollars a year.

Giving by rule has Bible sanction. Abraham gave one-tenth, and with God's blessing he became a man of princely fortune.

Jacob went out with his staff, a poor man. At Bethel he vowed to the Lord, "Of all that thou shalt give me I will surely give the tenth unto thee." In twenty years he came back rich.

St. Paul enjoins upon the Churches a weekly benefaction. "Upon the first day of the week let every one of you lay by him in store as God hath prospered him."

In no part of the work did John Wesley show more skill in handling his forces than in his class system. Each leader was to have the care of about twelve persons, not only looking after their spiritual needs as a sub-pastor, but receiving their contributions for the support of the Gospel and the poor. Every one who joined the Wesleyan Societies must give each week a due proportion of his income for the Lord's work. Wherever his plan was followed there was plenty of money for the needs of the Church.

In these times of financial pressure when so many of our benevolent enterprises are suffering heavy loss from the lack of means to push their interests, it would be well for us to go back to first principles in our finance. Let every child who comes into the Church as a probationer be taught that at least a penny a week must be given for the support of God's work. Let this be given regularly as an educator in beneficence. Let others give according to their means week after week, and the vexed questions of rented pews, begging speeches at dedications, agents, fairs and festivals would be happily settled to the infinite relief of many excellent people.

The Roman Catholics are ready enough to take up these plans and make them of the utmost avail. They have their Society for Propagandism, each member of which gives one cent a week. One collects from ten and forwards the dimes to another who sends the dollars to another, each collector gathering and forwarding from ten beneath him, till by the time it reaches the cardinal at Lyons it amounts to hundreds of thousands for pushing forward the plans of the Romish Church.

Papists never lack money. If a Protestant institution is to be sold for debt, Catholics have the money ready for its purchase, and that money is not from the bounty of the rich but from the littles given by the poor. It is high time for Protestants to begin to use the same wisdom in their financial plans.

When the *Woman's Foreign Missionary Society* was organized, many thought it a mistake that its constitution should forbid the taking of general collections. "So much interest in your meeting, ladies, such a tide of enthusiasm, surely if you would pass the baskets you would get hundreds of dollars." "Perhaps so, sir; but what about next year, when our fine talkers would not be here to stir the people? Better, far better as we believe, the plan of getting the women of the Church to lay aside, always religiously, the little two cents a week. The income will be larger and surer. And then as an educator of the people this society does more by inducing ten women to give a dollar a year, with the thought and prayer that usually accompany such gifts, than by persuading one to give a hundred dollars."

A thousand pities that all our benevolences might not be wrought by this same rule; each by a method of its own, but all upon the principle of gathering the littles steadily and constantly from the many.

But one says: "I am very poor. One-tenth of my income will be quite too insignificant to offer to the Lord." Let us not forget the widow of whom Christ said, "She hath cast in more than they all."

Let us be humble enough to give the little, and, though we can ill afford to spare it, let us trust as did the Gentile woman when required to take an extra boarder at the risk of starving herself and her children. God saw to it that her cruse of oil and barrel of meal did not fail. "But I am in debt." People have been known to keep up a lightning-rod of that sort to conduct off flashing appeals. I believe that if one would use the nine-tenths of his income, giving the other tenth to the Lord's work, he would get out of debt sooner than if he used upon himself the whole.

We measure our benevolence by that of others in the Church, when the fact is, the Church does not begin to give as she ought.

If she did, Christian enterprises would not be forever on the pauper list. Perhaps we are among the culpable. Let us face the facts in time, lest in the judgment the blood of the perishing be found upon us, lest our names be upon the roll of wrath.

Let us remember that our money, as an agent of good, belongs to our Master. Let us see to it that each dollar is spent under his eye. We may have his "Well done" on each business transaction, little and large. When they who have been won to him out of every kindred and tribe and people come up before him with joy, there may be those whom even our indirect efforts have helped on the way. Then will his word, sweeter than heaven's most glorious symphonies, sound through our souls. "Inasmuch as ye did it to one of the least of these my brethren, ye did it unto me."

GROWING OLD.

IN the evening twilight of each life there stand two grim, beckoning skeletons — age and death. We may laugh and shout in the merry to-day. We may dance and sing as did the condemned of the *Conciergerie* with the dead carts and coffins clattering up to the gate, and to-morrow—the guillotine! Yet we can not shut out the ghastly inevitable. There they stand— those grisly skeletons, age and death. We can escape the one only by the early coming of the other, from whom our every instinct draws back.

Age is as unsightly and probable as death is fearful and sure.

The physical havoc wrought by age is most unlovely and pitiful. If only the earthly house of this tabernacle could be taken down in a more dignified and agreeable manner, as probably it was intended at the outset!

See that old pair sitting in the chimney-corner. Once she was bright and beautiful; he handsome and brave. Now, they are wrinkled and bent and palsied. Her eyes were full of the passion and power of womanliness; his as keen as an eagle's glance. Now, the eyes of both are sunken and dim, seeing only blurs and blotches where once they traced beauty. Their hair, once heavy and dark, is coarse and gray, and tucked under uncouth skullcaps. Their teeth ached themselves away long since. Their limbs, that used to trip so nimbly and dance so gayly, have lost their sprightliness and strength. They can only totter and cramp and suffer rheumatic torture. Their hands have forgotten their cunning, and fumble as clumsily as do those of a twelvemonth's babe. Their voices have lost their melody and power; the poor old bodies whine out their ailments, and on sunny days croon and drawl about the dead past. Ah me! Is this skeleton reaching his arms for every one of us?

But sadder far than this physical decay is the failure of the mental powers. Once this man and woman were among the *élite*. Now, they set the youngsters a-titter with their old-fashioned whims and notions. "Mother's breaking fast," drawls the old man, nodding across at his wife. "A pity, too! She used to be wonderful smart, quite a blue stocking, as they used to say in my early days. Ah well, we've had our time."

One would care less for the tumbling down of the old tent, if the royal mind could stand unharmed in the wreck. The stout strokes of the good right arm, the deftness of the fingers, the strength and glory of the prime, could be given up, if the thought could yet be sent forth among men, a felt force. But to have book and pen fall from the palsied hand, and all the new developments of science and literature drift by unnoted, till one is as little *en rapport* with contemporary men and events as would be a resurrected Roundhead, thought and fancy cramped down to a little round of insignificant things, while the grand unfoldings of the age are as little comprehended as are the diplomacies of Thibet—who can contemplate such probabilities without a temptation to suicide?

Our old people in the corner remember when the business of the house and the estate were all wrought out in their brain. Now, their opinions are of little more weight than the guesses of the nimble-tongued ten-years-old. "Times are changed, father; they don't do things that way nowadays." "Why, mother, you are too old-fashioned for any thing."

Once that man's *ipse dixit* was authoritative in town affairs. Now, he urges a question that seems to him vital. Answer: "Why, father, that was settled years and years ago. Don't know as you can understand it, but it's all right. We got through with that the Winter before Bennie died. Don't you remember?" Yes, there are marble mile-stones that gleam, white and cold, like ghosts, along the misty, backward way; he can not lose sight of them; but all the rest seems like a fog-enshrouded sea.

Once his incisive thinking cut down through questions that concerned state interests, and his voice told on the destinies of the people. Now, he is cast aside, a child without the future of childhood, lacking all its sweetness and promise. With his worn-out body and effete mind, he is waiting in helplessness for the rickety, creaking machinery to stand still, and free him and his friends from the burden of his being.

And yet the picture has darker, sadder shades. Those people were once co-workers with the Lord Jesus Christ. Not only did they help nobly in reformatory movements, but they led many and many a soul to the Savior. Now, their religious life is as completely enfeebled as their mental vigor.

Their voices used to have weight in the councils of the Church. The pastor leaned upon them for sympathy and advice. Now, the Church moves on just as it would if they were in the grave. It works, legislates, extends, and they are unable even to comprehend its growth—in danger of reading it all backward. Well for them if they are not left to croak about the degeneracy of modern Christians. They can not pray and praise as they used to do. Things must have gone wrong some way. People have got out of the old paths. "When we were young you could tell a Christian woman by her bonnet as far as you could see her, and it would have done your heart good to hear how long and eloquent-like the men could hold forth in a meeting. But there were Christians in the Church in our young days."

Oh, the pity of it! To grow old! How many times, if we had dared, would we have prayed to die even before reaching "the half-way house" rather than come down to this whining, driveling, pushed-aside old life!

Is physical, mental, and moral decay inevitable? Is there no fountain of youth whose waters can give us immortal vigor?

Much of the decay of old age is the result of neglect, and, therefore, it may be avoided. In attempting to demonstrate this, perhaps, as in some people's theology, the wish is the parent of the argument, and the logic is not more robust than a wish, yet, as we all need comfort on this score, it may be worth while to make the effort to prove the proposition.

Lawlessness and laziness are the two prime enemies of human strength and endurance.

Unreasoning creatures live by law. The law of their life, though originally as benign as divine love could devise, has been infracted by man's sin, and carries the curse-mark of his transgression. Therefore they die. Their life moves in a circle. They come into existence, grow, mature, decline, and are crowded out of being by the pressure of on-coming successions. Except where the penalty of the curse comes in with ferocity and violence, these changes of the mode of being are, as far as we know, gentle, painless, and not unsightly. Who ever heard of a superannuated buffalo, or a chimney corner robin?

The ability to apprehend and obey law is the kingliness of humanity. It is the base of responsible action. It is that which recommended us to the redemptive notice of the Son of God. With our consent he will ultimately lift from us the curse. Even now he will help us mitigate the effects of that curse, but it must be according to law. Our perverse disposition to resist and break law is at the bottom of much of the misery that comes upon us when we grow old.

The taint of lawlessness is in our blood. It

comes to us straight from the forfeited paradise. It shows itself very early. Children hate restraint. Tell one of those " toddlin' wee things " not to touch a certain article, and he will not rest till his tiny fingers have pushed their way through your prohibition. The limitation suggests and stimulates the very mischief you would have him avoid. "What made you tell us not to put beans up our noses?" whined a little fellow, when his mother appeared on the scene of misdemeanor and suffering. "We wouldn't have thought of it if you hadn't 'a' told us not to."

In our childhood we could hop and skip all day, taking ten thousand useless steps, but it had to be at our own sweet will. If we were set at something that we felt obliged to do, our strength gave out immediately. You can "break" a colt in a month, but it takes ten years to break a boy to steady, reliable, working ways.

In mental effort also. Children's minds are uncomfortably busy, prying into every thing except their grammar and arithmetic. Pictures and prizes must be held before them perpetually, penalties and disgrace shaken over their heads, to coax or drive them into the habit of doing a required amount of work in a given time.

Many students make it the main task of their school life to resist, and wheedle, and outwit the teacher. He is their natural enemy. A harmless person, possibly, probably an amiable gentleman when they meet him in society, yet he represents the restraint of law, and, as such, must be beaten out of his purpose.

When they get the conduct of their life into their own hands, it is not unusual for them to throw the rein upon the neck of the lawless impulse. They do not venture to raise their hand against their neighbor's life for fear of the law of the land, and of the divine law that has been the one tireless schoolmaster that would not be shaken off; but may they not do as they will in regard to their own personal life? Their lawlessness relieves them of mental discipline, and they do no more brain work than they are driven to perform by necessity, or it permits them to indulge as they will their appetites, passions, ambitions. They destroy their digestion by crowding their stomachs to overwork upon fiery, greasy masses, villainous compounds that tickle a depraved palate, and that fill the blood with scrofula and fevers. They burn out their nerves and brain with the fumes of tobacco and alcohol.

If all this takes place among men who belong to Churches and claim to be governed by the Ten Commandments, what havoc of the life is made by those who have thrown off the restraints of the more special and personal of those injunctions!

Let us take an example of the habit of neglecting and one of observing physical and mental law—*Byron* and *Bryant.* The meteoric Byron indulged the worst passions. Bryant held himself to the simplest appetites and the purest personal life. Dissoluteness burned out the fuel meant to keep Byron's brilliant brain in force for years of glowing thought. Bryant lived by law, as do the beautiful, natural things about which he wrote so delightfully. He took ample sleep, and was up with the birds in the morning. His bill of fare was almost as simple as theirs— he breakfasted usually on oatmeal mush and milk. Byron was in the "sere and yellow leaf" when he was only a little over thirty. Bryant's age more than outmeasured two such rocket-flashes as Byron's erratic years. Seventy found him but little less agile in walking, climbing, leaping, indeed as young as at forty, except the few outer frost touches. Like Moses, he marched to his death with strength unabated.

The disgusting taint of physical and mental lawlessness and consequent decay renders odious and dangerous Byron's magnificent imagery. Bryant's poetry is as sweet and fresh and healthful as the breath of balm, and as restful as a mother's evening hymn.

Who would have his life like Byron's, flashing up luridly, and settling into murky night under the gloom of the disapproval of a more earnest time? How much better that it be like Bryant's, a strong, sure, steady light, ending like an Autumn day in calm glory, its rays slanting back over rich fruitage, and striking forward to a glorious dawn in the Morning Land!

Americans are in special danger of physical and mental degeneracy from fast living and overwork. Holmes says: "The human body is a furnace which keeps in blast threescore years and ten, more or less. It burns about three hundred pounds of carbon a year, besides other fuel, when in fair working order." We Americans are apt, as he says of pugilists, "to keep the vital fires burning with the blower up."

Strong, mixed blood bubbles in our veins, some of it the best of the Old World's life, driven hither because dangerous under rotten tyrannies. Below us heave the crowding masses. Before us stretch measureless possibilities. ·Forces push. Ambitions beckon, and on we go, with white lines about our mouths, and black furrows between our brows. We overwork and overdrive, and like the wicked, we do not live out half our days. We tire out and drop off to sleep under the sod coverlet before we have fairly reached our best working strength.

Albeit we would not exchange our civilization for that of the Norsemen, whose thick blood creeps through leathern veins, whose heavy jaws crunch the oaten cake, while their neutral-tinted faces are lighted dully with bovine comfort. No; they of the coming better time will feel to the full the propelling energy of this New World life; but they will live so by law, that they will not sin mortally against their physical being, and stretch themselves upon a bier just when they ought to be in the prime of vigor, their mental products inane sensualisms, when they ought to be full of power for the right.

The mind and spirit are princes. The body is a castle in which they stay threescore years or so. Their condition is often vitally affected by the good or ill repair of their habitation. In the earlier time the magnificence of the mansion eclipsed the dignity of the indwelling magnates. So now, often the greater care is given to polishing and strengthening the outer being. But the age of brawn is passing away, and the best thought is busy in bettering the spirit life. As usual, there is danger of swinging to the opposite extreme. Many good people underrate the influence of body upon soul, and serious harm comes of the blunder.

Bodies have rights that souls are bound to respect. They have ways of their own that are specially potent to avenge any infringement of right. If only a little finger is wronged, there may be an insurrection of pain that will set the whole system in a tumult, and throw even the kingly brain out of balance.

The years become relentless Eumenides to those who are reckless of physical law, stretching them upon the rack of acute suffering or the gridiron of slow torture. Witness the miserable old age of the dyspeptic and debauchee.

Many push their laudable purpose to secure a competency to such an excess that they destroy their ability to enjoy what they acquire.

The farmer thinks to wrest riches from the stingy soil by his own good right arm. He braves storm and weariness, he drives on through heat and cold, and finds himself at fifty a bent, stiffened, old man, with a cramped brain, a hungry soul, and, after all, only a few restless, unsatisfactory dollars.

The mechanic plays the same part with a slight change of scenery. The business man neglects all powers of body and mind except those that are necessary to the driving of a good bargain. When he grows old, whether he "fails" or "retires," he finds himself worn out and empty hearted, his faculty for love and worship dead almost beyond hope of resurrection.

The old Greeks took the very best care of their bodies. We see this illustrated in the Olympic games; the victor in running or wrestling was loaded with honor. When he returned to his city he was not permitted to enter through the gates, but a breach was made in the wall near his house, as if they would say, "The city that has such sons to guard her has no need of walls." The result was the finest physical culture, and consequent endurance. With them the age for military service was from twenty to sixty, and not, as with us, reaching only to forty-five.

We are as certainly culpable if we neglect to take care of our bodies as we are if we injure them by our excesses.

Many serve their bodies as rented houses are used. The roof leaks, the plaster begins to fall, the weather draws out the nails, and the clapboards spring off. No matter. We will not have to stay here long. Yes; but we had better be comfortable while we do stay, and not lose time and strength taking care of our coughs and rheumatisms.

Science, like religion, is growing wise and

practical. Instead of hiding away in midnight cells, straining every nerve to discover the undiscoverable, it has come into our homes and our schools, and is teaching us how to take care of our hair and teeth, our eyesight and digestion.

Hygiene miracles are wrought nowadays. Take dentistry, for instance. Years ago if the nerve of a tooth was injured, it was treated as some deal with refractory children. There was no inquiring into the cause of the trouble, no attempt at palliation or compromise. There was nothing for it, if it continued rebellious, after a few conciliatory pats and strokes, but to be exterminated, root and branch, though its loss could never be supplied.

Can we ever forget how, in our young days, the weeks and months were one protracted despair from toothache torture? Wedged in between the alternatives of the dentist's horrid steel and the prolonged agony of having those throbbing molars and incisors wear themselves out, one could almost have risked a Rip Van Winkle sleep, if he were sure of awaking toothless. We have learned of late, however, that a little daily care of the teeth and an early application of the dentist's skill will keep them in good condition for an indefinite period.

"Oh, but it is too much trouble. I have not time to bother with my teeth more than is absolutely necessary to cleanliness." Ah, that is a mischievous and expensive carelessness that you can ill-afford. You may save a few minutes by your neglect of the simple preventive, and, by and by, you may spend months upon the hot spit of agony, lose any amount of nervous vigor, and pay a good round bill for repairs.

A few years ago the papers told us how John Quincy Adams restored his eyesight by a little daily pressure upon his eyeballs. The old people looked at one another over their glasses and exclaimed, "Wonderful! How nice it would be to see once more without spectacles!" But I know of only one old lady who tried it perseveringly enough to restore her sight.

J. G. Holland tells us of an old gentleman, Dr. Scott, of Buffalo, who, when his eyesight began to fail, set himself about what he termed "ocular gymnastics." With proper intervals of rest, he exercised his eyes in making minute letters. At length he became able to read the newspapers without glasses; "and, at the age of seventy-one, he wrote upon an enameled card with a style on a space exactly equal to that of one side of a three-cent piece, the Lord's Prayer, the Apostles' Creed, the parable of the Ten Virgins, the parable of the Rich Man and Lazarus, the Beatitudes, the fifteenth Psalm, the one hundred and twentieth Psalm, the one hundred and thirty-third Psalm, the one hundred and thirty-first Psalm, and the figures 1860. Every letter and every punctuation mark was written exquisitely," "showing," as Dr. Holmes says of him, "that his eyes must be a pair of microscopes."

Much of the decay of old age comes from inactivity. Sometimes when a man finds that he has a competence, his ambition begins to lag, and he turns his business over to his sons. The relaxation of effort would have been disastrous at twenty-five—it is fatal at sixty. Unusual powers can not fail to lose their vigor.

The "childishness" of age is not inevitable; it may be prevented by mental hygiene. There is a close analogy between the laws of matter and those that govern mind. Neglect means decay. Inaction is paralysis. We have seen pictures of East Indian fakirs who had moved only one arm for a dozen years or more. That arm retained its strength, while the other limbs were no more under volitive control than if they had been made of wood. Most people treat the intellect in a similar fashion. They choose a business or profession, and throw all their mental force into the one faculty that is necessary to its successful management. The other faculties lie inactive till they become as useless as the limbs of the fakir. After a few years the need of using that one faculty ceases to crowd to activity. Then it falls into disuse and paralysis with the rest. The verdict is, "The old man has lost his mind." As Lowell says of a man minus his manhood, "A corpse crawls round unburied."

An accident or severe illness may injure the physical or mental constitution, and break up the ordinary or normal action of one's powers, yet usually we may work and be strong as long as we will.

Henceforth let us never say, "my memory is failing." Let us speak the plain truth: "Because I am not driven to use my memory as in my school-days I am neglecting it, and it is growing weak in consequence." A simple mnemonic exercise, the committing to memory of one text of Scripture a day, and the obliging of the mind to go over the whole of the chapter or book upon occasion will hold this faculty in vigor. If the memorizing of three hundred and thirteen dates, suggesting as many important points of history, one for each week-day of the year, were begun upon New Year's with a review once a week or once a month, a good knowledge of past events might be gained, and the memory would be held in strength by the discipline. This will be found to be an excellent exercise in a family, a thousand times better table-talk than the ordinary chitchat.

The terminology of any branch of natural science would make as good mnemonic gymnastics, helping the young people to a sure knowledge of what they certainly need to know, and keeping the older folk from degeneracy on account of the disuse of memory.

But one says, "I am so full of work and care I can not find time for mental discipline." We take time to eat because we can not live and keep our strength for work without food. If we must starve a part of our being, let it not be the nobler, the better, the immortal.

Where there's a will there's a way. Elihu Burritt mastered languages, science, literature, while supporting his family by working at his anvil.

Let the successful business man decide whether it will pay for a few paltry dollars more than his neighbor has the charge of, or a trifle better furnished house, or more elegant style of living, to cramp and dwarf his mind till he knows nothing but loss and gain and prices current.

Let the lady who never has time for study and thought weigh the matter fairly, and decide whether it will not be better for her to have a few pieces less of the twists and tangles of bright worsteds, a little plainer house-gear and simpler adornments for her person, and secure instead that sure, quiet strength of soul that will enable her to ward off the attacks of old age by and by.

Work or perish is the absolute law. When one begins to say, "I can not learn that, I am too old," his doom is sealed. Henceforth the chimney-corner! They who will work can keep their place in the ranks of workers in spite of of Time.

Humboldt wrote his "Kosmos" at fourscore. Isocrates finished one of his great works at ninety-seven. Theophrastus wrote his keen and sprightly "Characters" when a centenarian. Gorgias lived to the age of one hundred and seven, and died with the significant expression upon his lips, "Sleep is now beginning to lay me in the hands of his brother." Death came to Mary Somerville when she was ninety-two, and found her busy upon her abstruse and difficult astronomical mathematics — working her problems only a few hours before she fell asleep.

But the greatest, the saddest mistake is to imagine that the years must dull our devotional fervor, cripple our spiritual powers, and destroy our usefulness. It is a trick of Satan to crowd out of the ranks those who have the best equipment for service—a ripe, full Christian experience.

God has said, "I will never leave thee, nor forsake thee." Does not that include the whole of probation? "My grace is sufficient for thee, for my strength is made perfect in weakness." Does not that cover all our infirmities? "Lo, I am with you alway, even unto the end of the world." Does not his presence insure constant development and growing usefulness?

I remember a beautiful woman who could hardly have been lovelier in any of her life than in the last years, when she was over ninety. She entertained us at the piano with music that she composed sixty years before. She was fully in sympathy with all the aggressive work of good people, and kept pace in her prayers and faith with each movement. "I can't go to your missionary meeting to-night," she said in her sweet, simple way, as we were starting to our anniversary," but I will try and help a little here at home."

"I knew you'd have a good meeting," she said, when we returned, her face aglow with the glory of the world beyond. "My heart was so warm when I talked to the Master about your work." Who can tell which rendered the most helpful service that night, we at the church, or she in her room "talking to the Master?"

As sunset hours are usually the most glorious of the day, so the last years ought to be, of all, most replete with beauty and excellence, rich with the ingatherings of time and the foreshadowings of the blessedness that is soon to be revealed. "The hoary head is a crown of glory if it be found in the way of righteousness."

For what a glorious, eternal garnering may one hope who has spent a long life in the service of the Master.

www.ingramcontent.com/pod-product-compliance
Lightning Source LLC
Chambersburg PA
CBHW031748230426
43669CB00007B/538